Mama Says...

...When A Wolf Is Chasing You, Throw Him A Biscuit But Don't Stop To Bake Him A Cake.

A Chronicle Of Motherly Advice Across Continents And Cultures And In Between

Maria L. Valdemi

Creative Director
Louis A. Cannizzaro

Designer
Chris Klimasz

L.A.C. Communications, Inc.

To All Good Mothers Everywhere

*Much have
I seen and known,*

*I am a part of
all that I have met.*

— *Alfred Lord Tennyson*

Table of Contents

"A mother tells you things,
sometimes over and over and over.
She can sum up life in 25 words
or less."

About Mothers...
Mine and Yours...
The Common Thread.

These stories begin in New York City with my mother, Anna Stagliano, and branch out across the world. They begin with her words, the words that she shared with me. My mother's world was vast, her own particular circle of life, which encompassed all that she met.

Her stories and sayings were tied to a common thread which connects us all. We all have our stories, our sayings and our own family and friends that form our circles of life. It is these stories and these sayings that keep us interconnected and form the world.

When my mother died ten years ago, I had some clothes and some pieces of jewelry she left. I had the old photographs and the old memories, both happy and sad. The most important treasures, however, were her words and stories.

A mother belongs to all times, to all cultures. Whether she is personified by a Renaissance Madonna or the frayed edges of our own worn photographs, she is the first and, oftentimes, greatest influence in life.

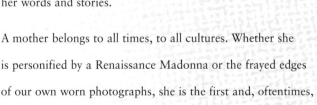

A mother tells you things, sometimes over and over and over. She can sum up life in 25 words or less. She can express the same thought in 25 different ways.

And I remembered the people in my particular circle of life who have influenced me. They come from many places and cultures. Although the stories and sayings they expressed are different, depending upon the people or the language, they all describe eternal truths. Some are happy. Some are sad. All ring true.

Each mother has a story and each mother has had an influence upon me, those I love, and you. Like some vast infinity, we started in different places yet we have arrived at exactly where we were meant to be.

As I began to record the stories and words of my family and friends, I decided to enlarge the circle and reach out to those whom I admire. And the stories that began in New York City were enriched with a poetry recitation by Billy Collins, the Navajo world of artist, R. C. Gorman, the literary remembrances of Tony Hillerman, the tales of bluesman, Fruteland Jackson and the maternal advice given to Donald Trump for both business and life.

In their stories and sayings, I realized that a mother is any or all women with whom life and experiences are shared. A mother, like her words, is universal. These stories and sayings cross continents and cultures.

A mother's life, like all lives, is measured in years. A mother's love is endless, sometimes recalled with a turn of a phrase. Evoking a smile, a laugh or a tear, these words transcend time.

I still hear my mother's stories and sayings—25 at a time, in 25 different ways—over and over and over. I have written some of them down for you and for me. The world that began in New York City has grown to encompass a world, my world.

Although we may now know each other, we are all connected. We have our own stories and sayings. And all of our worlds, both yours and mine, bring us closer to each other, closer than we think we are.

*"The winds of March
carry the scents of spring."*

About Me...

My life of words began in New York City. My twin
brother and I were born there. Our address was 1667
Lexington Avenue, a place that exists only within the
borders of black and white photographs. New York
City was our first home and our block consisted
of a melange of Cubans, Germans, Hungarians,
Italians and Jews.

One of my first unforgettable sayings was not
uttered by my mother but by Pauline and Davey
Berkowitz, neighbors in our apartment building.
Each time they saw us, no matter how many
times a day, they put their hands on top of our
heads and prayed aloud--
"Something, something keppela." Years later,
I learned they were asking God for a blessing
on our little heads, a blessing, just for us.

"A blessing on my head"

1667 Lexington Avenue was a magic place for me. There were
picnics in Jefferson Park, the feast of Our Lady of Mt. Carmel,
the bakery on 102nd Street, Italian ices and the unforgettable
array of aromas and accents that framed my world. Sounds
of Spanish, English and Yiddish punctuated that world,
a world that existed for a mere five years.

5

My father, Luigi, was born in Genova. He was happy
in New York City. My mother never liked the city, nor
apartment dwelling.

My mother loved the country and wanted her own house and
garden. Neither my father nor my brother nor I had any say in

the decision. Mama packed up the entire
family including our dog, Fido, and took
us to the only place my father could
afford. Stony Point was a very rural
place in those days, a place with no
aromas, accents, or Italian Ices.

Maria, Papa and Gino Carlo

I recall our first night in our tiny house. As darkness descended,
I went out to the back steps and gazed at a large tree. There in
our backyard I saw the faint outline of an animal, hanging from
its tail on the lowest branch.

Never having seen such a sight, I began to shout and my mother
ran out to the steps. I pointed toward the opossum and then
hid my face in Mama's skirt. Gently she turned me toward the
tree and Mama said that I had to learn to live with it because
the animals were here first. I spent the entire night staring
out the window, spying rabbits, raccoons and deer.

Our street soon filled with neighbors: the Wilsons, the
Miglionicos, the Giffens and the Kingmans. No one ever

kept a door locked and everyone was welcome in everyone
else's home. It was a street where neighbors did for each
other without thought of repayment. It was a street where
neighbors cared for each other without thought of repayment.

And so I began my adventures. Sometimes alone, other times
accompanied by some incredible people.

Houses were sold and new people came.
The Bulsons, the Lindbergs, the Ramundos
and Chuck Mayer joined our special family
of neighbors. I have been fortunate. All those
blessings on my "keppela" have served me well.

My Brother, Gino Carlo

I cherish all the people I have known, all the people I have met.
Some are with me. Some are long gone.

Two, however, stand above the rest: my parents.
While they lived, I never knew how extraordinary they were.

My mother remains with me. I can't always see her in my mind.
I can't always remember days and events. Memories of birthdays
and holidays and Christmases past have all merged into black
and white photographs. I will never find 1667 Lexington Avenue
again. That array of aromas and accents is gone.

What I have are my mother's words. Even now I hear her.

"To wash the head of the donkey is to lose water, soap and time."

Anna Stagliano Valdemi, My Mama

My mother was beautiful. She was the most talented person I've ever met. She could do anything. She could also be the most infuriating person on the planet.

Maria, Mama and Gino Carlo

When we were born in Mother Cabrini Hospital, the doctors advised her to take the little girl home. Leave the little boy, Gino Carlo, in the hospital for he was hopelessly brain damaged and would die. But, she brought us both home and the hopeless little boy lived for 28 years.

She loved him more than anything or anyone. He was not a burden to her. He gave her unconditional love and a reason for living.

On our street she was a mama to all. Her advice was always sought after and she cared for everyone who needed her. Whether it had two legs or four, she was mama.

Maria and Gino Carlo

When we were about eight years old, my brother became severely ill with pneumonia. Mama went to the hospital to be with him. My father had to get me ready for school in the morning and have dinner ready at night.

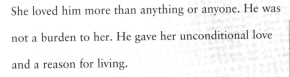

9

He was never a great cook and both Fido and I refused to eat.
In the dog's case, however, it was not completely about the food.
Fido was used to being fed by my mother and she was not there.
One day went by and then another, and he did not see her.
Although I myself gave Fido his food, the dog refused to eat.
So my mother came home from the hospital each day to feed
him. Both the dog and my brother survived.

It was not easy growing up in our house. There were many
expectations and many wishes to be fulfilled. And there was
always my brother and the thought that had he been given my
life, he would have achieved far more than I.

Sunday in the park: Fido, Mama, Gino Carlo and Me

My relationship with my mother was complex, filled with love and anger and recriminations. She remained the lifelong matriarch of the family, an inflexible part to assume, a sometimes inflexible person to approach. It was only with her death that I could put aside the "mother" role and see the person. As she lay dying, she kept repeating that, as a child, she had been sent to live with relatives.

She kept repeating that her mother had given her away, that her mother had not wanted her. My only response was to reassure her that it had happened a long time ago, that it was not happening now and that I wanted her. Each night I told her that I loved her but she met my words with silence.

Suddenly the decision she had made so many years before in Mother Cabrini Hospital came full circle. My mother could not allow her son to die alone, as if abandoned and unwanted. My hopelessly brain damaged brother was part of her and she could never give him away to strangers. Even if the whole world did not want him, she did.

He was her son, neither hopeless, nor brain damaged. To her, he was beautiful, a gift from God. Life was cruel to Anna yet she stood up to it like steel. Life could not shatter her. Life could not defeat her. Her faith in God never wavered. All those

Night by R. C. Gorman

months I nursed her, all those months I took care of her are difficult to describe or to express. There is a lithograph, called "Night" by the great artist R. C. Gorman that sums up our relationship.

It depicts two women clothed in long white shawls. The woman on the viewer's left is old and, possibly dying.

Her head is on the shoulder of a younger woman, possibly her daughter. The young woman is watching over her, with great tenderness and strength.

I am not my mother, although there is a part of her in me. I, too, had assumed an inflexible part to play. After her death, I put aside the "daughter" role.

My mother's death gave me freedom. My mother's death gave me the strength to live my own life.

There was no more mother, no more daughter. There was no anger, no need for recriminations. I am Maria. She was Anna, my mama.

Now, I remember the love.

Mama and Me

CALABRIA

My Mama was born in Pittsfield, Massachusetts. The first 13 years of her life, however, were spent in a small town called Borgia, in the province of Calabria. The Calabresi are equally known for their stubbornness ("testaduri" or hardheads) and their generosity.

Mama told me many stories about Borgia. Her family was poor but she managed to go to public school and to attend the convent school where she learned to sew. At the mercy of her wicked aunts, she always boasted that she was an American and would someday return to her homeland.

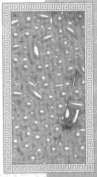

Mama's pearls of wisdom

Although she never spoke of Borgia with any affection, she would recall a few memories, always associated with the holidays. On Christmas Eve, the shepherds came down from the hills to lead the procession to the church. All kept time to the music of the bagpipes. Christmas Eve supper was not complete without 13 different foods on the table, the main course, baccala. Easter was my favorite because Mama made her braided Easter Bread, the "Cuzuppa". The year she died, she passed the recipe to me.

Calabria is the heel and toe of Italy, a province of oaks and pines and rocks and blue sea. It has witnessed countless invaders from Greeks to Albanians to Arabs and Normans and

Spaniards. My mother left Borgia in 1933 and she never returned. Yet in her heart she kept the traditions of Calabria.

These are the words of Calabria as expressed by my Mama and delivered with equal doses of stubbornness and generosity.

Mama's earrings and to the right, Mama's gold chain and medallion, her most valued pieces of jewelry

Whenever Mom gave me advice as to how to do something or other, I often ignored it. She never said *"I told you so"* but...

"To wash the head of the donkey is to lose water, soap and time."

I have found this one is universal...

"Tell me who you're with and I'll tell you who you are."

When Mama heard of someone with a blessing that was undeserved, she would say....

"God gives bread to those who have no teeth."

If a wealthy person won a lottery or got more than his share of good luck, Mama would say...

"Money sticks to money."

MAMA
SAYS

Quite a few times, I went out with guys she did not think were worthy of her baby. After the break up, Mama would observe...

"Better to be alone than to be miserable with someone."

The native costume of Calabria

This one is a particular favorite...

"If you want to be happy in marriage, marry an orphan.

My brother and I were both born in March and she loved to say about us...

"The winds of March carry the scents of spring."

15

My mother's sister, Aunt Lucy, was only
18 months younger than Mama.
They loved each other very
much but they battled royally.
If she lost an argument
with Aunt Lucy, she
would comment...

"Always agree with a madman."

And sometimes in a backhanded compliment,
Aunt Lucy got the following...

"Even a madman can speak wisely."

Mama had many sayings for love...

"The heart cannot be commanded."

"True love can't be bought or sold."

"There is no love without sorrow."

ANNIE'S KITCHEN

As Queen of her kitchen, no one dared to interfere or to comment when she was cooking. Surrounded by some of her favorite utensils, Annie's kitchen was the heart of her home.

Life was not always good to my mother and yet she never complained. Mama would just shake her head and say...

"Better to take the world as it comes."

"Who is content with what he has is a winner."

Mama on friendship...

"A friend to everyone is a friend to no one."

"Who does good receives good."

"It's easier to be wise for others than to be wise for oneself."

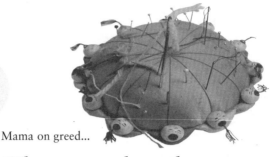

Mama on greed...

"The more you have, the more you want."

"Where your treasure is, there is your heart."

Each time I have to attend an event where I really don't want to be or have to show up for some occasion that is a nuisance, I always hear my Mama saying...

"Better a piece of bread and an onion in peace than a grand feast in miserable company."

My mother and father were married for 48 years and they had their share of arguments. This is another great one about marriage...

"The hen lays the eggs but it's the rooster's ass that burns."

As I frequently get into trouble for stating my opinion,

I remember Mama smiling…

"Keep your eyes open and your mouth closed."

"He who does not know is like he who does not see."

I had my share of discouragements and

she would say…

"Never say never."

Her philosophy of life can be summed up this way…

"As long as there is life, there's hope."

THE THREE
LITTLE KITTENS

Mama learned to sew as a child and she could sew as well as she could cook. When I was 5, she struggled to teach me to embroider this humble work of art. For years, the piece was missing in action. After her death, I discovered it in her special drawer, hidden away and prized as one of her most valuable possessions.

"I'm not a thinker
but everything they said was right."

R. C. Gorman

I first saw the art of R. C. Gorman 16 years
ago. After attending a writer's conference, I wandered
through the alleys of Taos, New Mexico. On Ledoux
Street, I found his gallery. When I walked through
the doors, I entered a world of beauty.

With meager financial resources, my only purchase
was a poster called Zia. A beautiful woman, swathed
in white, is sitting on the ground. She is one with
the land and she is part of all that surrounds her.

R. C. Gorman
with his cat Peggy Sue

In Italian, "Zia" means "Aunt" and the woman reminded
me of my Aunt Lucy. She had gone to Argentina and was
no longer a part of my life.

I missed her so much and the poster captured the love I felt
for her. Six years later, after the death of my mother,

MUSÉE MUNICIPAL DE SAINT-PAUL
R.C. GORMAN
du 9 Mai au 4 Juin 1979

Zia by R. C. Gorman

I again trekked to Taos. In
that gallery on Ledoux Street,
I came upon the lithograph,
"Night." All the pain, all the
hurt that I was still carrying
seemed to lift from my soul.
Death had not taken my
mother from me. Death had

placed her at my side where she will always be.

And so, when pondering whom to approach for my book, I thought of R. C. Gorman. I wrote to the gallery, asking only for a quote or a paragraph about the artist's mother and his mother's family, for Navajo society is matrilineal. What I received from R. C. and Virginia Dooley, the Gallery's director, was an invitation to lunch and, and even more important, the chance to spend time with someone I admire.

R. C. Gorman was born in Chinle, the heart of Dinetah, the land between the sacred mountains. It was here that his first designs were made in the spring clay, his first sketches on rocks. Traveling with his grandmother and her flock of sheep through Dinetah, he regards his childhood as blessed.

Night Stories by R. C. Gorman

His grandmother was tall and beautiful. She taught him the stories and traditions of the Dine, the Navajo word for "the people". The women not only maintained their homes, or hogans, but also took care of the children, the sheep and the tracts for grazing. In Navajo society, women are the caretakers of the universe.

R. C. remembers setting up camp and observing his aunts
making tortillas, fried potatoes and mutton stew.
His grandmother would make cheese in a coffee can, shred
it into pieces and fry it along with Navajo bread. It was
the future gourmet's favorite treat.

Adele, his mother, worked off the
reservation and it was she who
brought R. C. his first sheets of paper.
She saved these first drawings, done
when he was just three years old.
Today they are a part of his private
collection, proudly displayed
next to other works of art by
Tamayo, Picasso, Dali and Zuniga.

His first drawing

It was his grandmother, however, who taught him that work
was important. She was his favorite lady. He still recalls her
sheep and her spotless white donkeys. He recalls how his
aunts prepared the traditional foods and stored them for
winter. And they always had time to tell a story and to
show him how to work with clay.

In the land between the sacred mountains, the boy realized
that he could create. Helping his aunts and his grandmother,
R. C. became aware of a sense of community. He relied upon
these strong women and he worked alongside them, becoming

part of the natural order. When I asked him about any particular bits of maternal wisdom, he laughed and said, "I'm not a thinker but everything they said was right."

When World War II came, his father Carl was assigned to a group called the Navajo Codetalkers. His mother decided that R. C. had to go to school and learn the ways of non-Navajo society. His first introduction to Catholic boarding school was a disaster. Narrow-minded and mean-spirited, the nuns punished Navajo children for speaking their own language. R. C. was forced to shovel coal as punishment and hunger was his constant companion.

While Navajo Codetalkers were helping to win the war, many who remained in the community were sequestered behind barbed wire fences alongside German prisoners of war. R. C.'s mother, however, saved enough money to send her son to Ganado, to the Presbyterian School.

At Ganado, the Navajo language was encouraged. The Gospels were spoken in Navajo and it was R. C.'s grandmother who translated the hymns which are still sung. During holidays he stayed and worked to help pay his tuition.

R. C. was free to draw but he told me that no art school can teach you to be you. Art is basically an expression of the artist. Art is an expression of who you are. Art opens the world to you.

After a stint in the Navy, he attended Northern Arizona
University. In 1958 he went to Mexico and discovered the
works of Rivera, Orozco, Siqueiros and Zuniga.
He saw their awesome murals and received a
grant to study in Mexico. He came in contact
with artists who depicted their own people, who
saw beauty in their own people.

When R. C. returned, he set up a studio in San Francisco.
He supplemented his income by modeling and began
experimenting with different styles of art. When told that
his work resembled Zuniga, he changed his style. Awareness
of his work brought him awards and brought him to Taos.

He arrived in the middle of the night. When he awoke the
next morning and saw all the beauty around him, he knew
that Taos was the place for him.

R. C.'s favorite subject is women.
He surrounds himself with
women. His home is alive with
family, friends and a cat named
Peggy Sue.

A sassy Peggy Sue

One of his aunts still visits. His beloved housekeeper and
companion, Rose, died in 2002. R. C. maintains a
shrine to her.

He generously shares his talents
with fellow artists. For the past
26 years, he has been assisted by
Joseph Sparks, a multi-talented artist
in his own right. Joseph is Rose's son.
All he wants from life is to pass on
his learning to children.

Joseph Sparks

R. C. Gorman opened his home to us, wined and dined us
and told us we were free to take pictures and use them in this
book. As I walked from room to room, and then sat and spoke
with him, I sensed circles all around me. I felt a connection
to everything.

He creates a world with just a few lines. A bare outline, just a
few fluid lines, depict a mother and child, or one woman or
many women. They represent all that is important to him.

We are all connected in a vast, perhaps infinite, circle. Through
our grandmothers, our aunts, and our mothers, we are a part of
life and a part of the earth from which we all came and to which
we must, ultimately, return.

In the artist's company, I sensed that where I was in that circle
of life was the most important place for me to be. When I
asked him to sum up his art, he looked around and said,
"Well, it's there and I want more people to see it."

R. C. lives in three worlds, three circles of life. He lives in
the world of his grandmother and aunts, the world of the
Dine. His mother, who spoke only English to him, brought
him into the non-Navajo world. And, through his creations,
a third world of beauty has been created, a world that touches
all who experience his work.

The Navajo believe that the circle of life has neither beginning
nor end. The world can only exist in harmony and balance.
Both gods and mortals have emerged from four previous
worlds. The four clans of the Navajo were created by
Changing Woman, who is both chief deity and their common
ancestor. This present world is the fifth world and the last.

R. C. Gorman has added another dimension to this fifth world,
his own art. There is beauty everywhere in his work. He
has made his circle wide enough for all of us to share his art.

I studied the walls of his home. There were paintings,
drawings, lithographs, etchings and papercasts. I glanced at
the grand piano topped with the bronze cast of his father.
I walked into his garden and touched sculptures, mobiles and
Joseph's totem poles. I saw with my eyes and I saw
with my soul.

In art I can feel truth. I can live and walk in the world
of R. C. Gorman.

Suddenly I remembered the words of a Navajo prayer:

With Beauty Before Me

With Beauty Behind Me

With Beauty Below Me

With Beauty Above Me

With Beauty All Around Me

Daughter Of The Moon, by R. C. Gorman

R. C. is part of the Dine circle of life that includes his grandmother, his mother and his aunts. In this world, we find harmony, balance and beauty. And I knew that in that moment and in this place, R. C. Gorman was the personification of that prayer.

R C gorman

29

*"Your children will return all the
love and happiness you give them."*

Argentina

Lucia Nazira Rezck

This mama was born on March 20, 1940 in
Rivadavia, in the province of Mendoza, Argentina.
Her father was Syrian and her mother was Argentinian.

Her earliest memories are of a devoted family,
including 14 uncles who gathered every Sunday
at her Grandmother Lucia's house for dinner and

Lucia by the Sea

discussion. These family repasts were as full of fun
and rowdiness as any scene imaginable with 14 uncles
who had, at least, 14 different political opinions.

Her childhood seemed charmed with a family that supported
her every step. From them, Lucia learned to trust. She learned
to believe in herself and to set her aim toward the heavens.

Attractive and talented, Lucia was a beauty
queen at 19, representing the city of
Rivadavia. She married and gave birth to
her first child, Viviana. Pedro followed in
1964. She then moved the family to Buenos
Aires to care for her brother, Emilio, who
had been diagnosed with cancer. He did not
recover. He died in her arms and she would
later confess that his death was the greatest
tragedy of her life.

Beauty Queen of Rivadavia

Still yet, there were other misfortunes. In Buenos Aires, her husband left her, but Lucia did not spend a minute moaning or groaning. She had two children to raise and she would provide them with a loving home. She taught piano and worked in biochemistry. She worked days and she worked nights but she never lost hope.

In February 1970 she married again. Her third child, Lizi, was born in 1971. Her second husband also abandoned the family but she never spoke a word of recrimination against either man. She taught her children to respect their fathers, even though they played no significant roles in their upbringing.

Viviana, Pedro and Baby Lizi

The family reunited around Lucia and her children. She was a woman who loved life and always had a smile on her face. She loved sharing her life with friends and family. She took on extra employment so that she could afford to take her three children on holiday trips.

In 1989, Lucia bought a house in Ituzaingo, a suburb of Buenos Aires. Here, her daughter Lizi met my cousin, Mauricio. They married and our family roots, which extend from Liguria and Calabria to New York and Massachusetts and California, now stretch through South America.

When Lucia and Lizi came into our family, they brought a new song, a new tempo to our family history. Within a year, Mauro was born and Lucia spent every day with him. Five brief months later, with no warning, Lucia died of a cerebral aneurysm. Her last words, "I have been reborn" still comfort Lizi.

Many people came to pay their respects and each of them had an anecdote or a story to tell about Mama Lucia. One said that she remembered that her greatest bit of advice was not to hate, neither friend nor foe. To hate is a waste of time.

Others said that Lucia was a source of strength to them because she helped all who sought her assistance. She always believed in people, in their talents and in what they could achieve. She believed in the goodness of people. And others whispered that they could not believe that the beautiful woman with the beautiful eyes and the sweet smile would no longer be part of their lives.

Yet Lucia is part of their lives. She always told Lizi that life goes on, and it does. Life can neither be impeded nor stopped. A year later, Lizi gave birth to her second child, Mati.

Mauricio, Mauro, Lizi and Mati

Lucia was like a star that burns bright and fast. Not everyone may have seen it and known it, but all those who did will never forget its brilliance. She lives on in her children, her grandchildren, and in her words.

33

ARGENTINA

A magnificent country of waterfalls, mountains, pampas and icebergs, Argentina is also a nation of immigrants. Part of my family is there, too. After the Second World War, my mother's youngest sister, Marianna and her husband, Domenico immigrated to Buenos Aires with their three children, Giovanna, Gregorio and Jose.

Mate, the national drink, beverage and cure-all of Argentina

Argentina is represented by gauchos, soccer and polo players, tango singers and dancers. For me, it is a place where a part of my family resides and, therefore, I cherish it.

Here, a Mama raised her children. She gave them her love, her strength and her words to remember.

This is one of the best definitions of life that I have ever heard...

> **"We have to love people
> with all their defects and virtues.
> Learn to forgive and
> forget, so you won't be alone in life."**

The Gaucho, like our cowboy of the West, symbolizes freedom and evokes legends.

Whenever Mama Lucia gave a donation to charity, she would say...

> **"God will pay me back by
> giving health to my grandchildren."**

34

She worked many jobs to support her family and she

taught them never to ridicule any form of work

or worker...

**"Believe that all work is honorable
and it will never become a burden
or a sacrifice."**

*A hand carved flute
from the province of
Misiones*

This was her philosophy about labors in life...

**"Work is a tool
that helps us enjoy life."**

*La Companera
rode with the Gaucho
and was as rugged
and self-
sufficient as the
cowgirls of the West.*

When Lizi had her first child Mauro, her mother

gave her this advice...

**"Your children will return
all the love and happiness
you give them."**

Although she suffered a great deal,

this was her philosophy of life...

**"In spite of the sorrows and
tribulations, life is beautiful."**

"When you die, the house remains behind and you're still dead."

Yolanda Aramendi

Yolanda is my best friend in Stony Point. She moved into her house in 1993, the year my parents died. A widow, she came with her mother, Mamacita, more formally known as Blanca Consuelo Gomez.

We did not meet until the spring of 1994. It was April or May and, in my mother's memory, I decided to tackle her garden. I had never even touched a weed or turned over a handful of soil. However, I was determined, so with gardening tools and my CD player in hand, I entered the backyard.

Yolanda celebrating her 15th birthday

The first order of business was to put on some music. For this horticultural foray, I chose Beniamino Gigli, the great Italian tenor. As the magnificent arias colored the air, Yolanda peeked outside her door. She introduced herself as a fellow opera lover and we have been friends from that moment.

Yolanda, shopping in Havana

Yolanda and Mamacita became part of my life. We exchanged stories and Mamacita would tell me about her adventures. She was born in Burgos, Spain, one of 15 children. At the tender age of nine, Mamacita and the Gomez Family settled in Cuba.

37

Her father owned land in Cuba but tragedy struck when Papa Gomez was swindled by his own brother of almost all that he owned. The disgrace shattered him and he took his own life.

Now a widow, Blanca's mother was left with 14 children, ranging in ages from 21 to 3. The oldest and the youngest children were parceled out to Catholic boarding schools. Blanca and the five in the middle range remained at home. She always remembered the day her siblings left, hand-in-hand and crying, for they did not know when they would see each other again.

At 13, Blanca became the surrogate mother for the children. She even had to care for her own mother who now suffered from depression. Blanca cooked, cleaned, sewed and kept the family intact.

Yolanda and Xavier

When she was 21, she met the love of her life, Valentin Rodriguez. Born in La Palma, the Canary Islands, he had immigrated to Cuba in 1920. They had two children, Yolanda and Margarita. Valentin went to work for Bacardi® and had a very interesting clientele.

One of the districts of Havana that was part of his territory was a place called San Francisco de Paula. Yolanda recalls that it was the place where you could buy the best cupcakes in all of Cuba. And it was a big adventure to get into

Cuba

the car and drive through San Francisco de Paula.

As they would pass through the residential section, Yolanda's
father would point to the crest of the hill and tell them that
although they could not see it, there was a house at the top
called La Vigia. It was the house of one of his clients, a man
to whom he personally delivered cases and cases of rum.
He could not drive up whenever he wanted. He had
to make a special appointment to get into La Vigia.

Yolanda and Margie, however, were interested in getting to
the cupcakes. Although they knew that this was the house
of "Senor Ernesto" and that he was a famous writer, the
cupcakes took precedence. Hemingway was probably more
interested in visiting his favorite bar in the neighborhood,
La Bodeguita del Medio, a place where he had a seat of
honor. No one was allowed to sit in the spot where he
imbibed his daily daiquiri.

In 1955, it was Yolanda's father who realized that he had to
get his family out of Cuba. They chose to leave their
homeland rather than live under a dictatorship. Yolanda and
Margie came to the United States. At first, Yolanda attended
boarding school in the Pennsylvania Dutch Country. These
were lonely times until the family was finally reunited and
came to live in the borough of Queens, a section of
New York City.

Mamacita had a great way of raising her daughters. Because she did not want them to be slaves to the kitchen or the house, she did not teach them anything about cooking and cleaning. She told them that eventually they would learn all that they needed to know about running a household, but in life, the important thing was to be educated, to be able to make your own way and never be dependent upon anyone.

In Queens they made a new life. Margie married Iggy and had two children, Loretta and Joseph. Yolanda met her future husband, Xavier, a Basque, and there in Queens, they were married. Too soon, he died.

Over our backyard fences we discussed and debated the mysteries of life. Our commentaries were not complete without Mamacita. She had a smile that could dazzle the sun. Spanish, Italian and English flew through those hours that we passed together.

As we tended our gardens, we exchanged gossip and ideas. We spent holidays together and savored our special holiday foods. There were always bags and boxes going from one house to the other and over the fences.

And this became a quandary for me. After my parents died, I was all set to sell our house and go anywhere. (Actually, it was a toss up between Santa Fe, New Mexico and Italy.) But over these past 10 years, each season has turned into another and I am still here in my mother's house.

One of the reasons for staying is that Yolanda is only
one house away. Mamacita is gone now
but whenever I step into my backyard I
can feel her. In each flower I can see a
trace of her smile.

Mamacita and Yolanda

Although our houses have their share of
memories, we are making new ones.
Yolanda attended my wedding and I am a part
of her family. She cares for me just as she cares
for her sister and her nieces and nephews.

We cherish each other. Yolanda and I discuss El Cid and Spain
and Cuba in the old days. I tell her my father's stories, my mother's
stories and I tell her what Stony Point was like 50 years ago.

We cherish our old photographs and gaze at them for hours.
We share our love of music and travel and, sometimes,
we travel to Yolanda's basement and listen to old phonograph
records — yes, records, of the tango.

We speak with each other every day. We take care of each
other's animals. We watch each other's house. We go shopping.
We sometimes "do lunch." And at home, over espresso,
we pour out our souls to each other.

Someday I will leave but wherever I go, I'll not find a
friend like Yolanda.

CUBA

A beautiful island, surrounded by the bluest ocean, is the way
Yolanda remembers her homeland. Havana was a jewel, a city
of boulevards, lined with buildings that ranged from colonial
architecture to art nouveau.

Enfolded in an extended family that included grandparents, aunts
and uncles and cousins, Yolanda's childhood was filled with music,
tropical breezes, great food and love. Her favorite meal was

Mamacita's roast pork with yucca and black beans with rice.
Yolanda has spent more time in the United States than she
ever spent in Cuba. These years have been a time of exile
for she has not been able to return to her homeland.

*A cherished keychain
is the symbol of a
lost homeland.*

The great Cuban poet, Jose Marti, expressed the sentiment
that when he died he wished to be buried with a bouquet of
flowers and a flag from his homeland. When you leave the
country of your birth, a part of you remains there. When
you are forced to leave the country of your birth, a part of
it remains in your heart, in your soul, in your words.

Having grown up with a father who knew Ernest Hemingway
and valued the world of literature, education and self-improvement
have always meant a great deal to Yolanda...

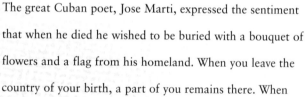

"He who gets close to a good tree gets good shade."

42

Yolanda is very active and I think she lives by this particular phrase...

"Never put off until tomorrow what you can do today."

I can just hear Mamacita saying this about housework...

"When you die, the house remains behind and you're still dead."

Here are two on marriage...

"He who gets married desires his own house."

"When you marry, you don't marry a person — you marry a family."

Whenever I am in need of consolation and it seems as if there's no answer, Yolanda gives me a hug and whispers...

Cigars are the most famous export of Cuba.

"God never gives you more than you can handle; He may strangle you but He never kills you."

"When God closes a door, He opens another."

"It's not the robes that make the king."

Poland

Sabina Pajak

This mama was born in 1940 in Belarussia.
As Polish nationals, her family was forced to relocate
in 1945. After the war, another world had been
created. New maps had been drawn and new borders
now separated families from families and friends
from friends.

*Sabina and
Grandchild, Zoe*

The Pajak family were farmers and tended their
land and their fruit orchard. Sabina was the second
youngest in a family of seven, and all the children
had to work to maintain the farm.

Despite the aftermath of war, her childhood memories
were happy ones. Her mother was a reticent woman and did
not believe in extravagances, not that they had any to spare.
Her one love of beauty was expressed in the traditional
Easter eggs that she hand-decorated every season.

Sabina's father was the love of her life.
She remembers that he could make a treasure out
of anything, the proverbial silk purse from a sow's
ear. He collected little tin cans and decorated them.
He filled them with berries. He bought candies to
top off the cans and gave them as gifts to his children.

Polish Crest

She recalls that their house had stained glass windows and, after all these years, still recalls their beauty. Christmas Midnight Mass followed by a great, early breakfast was the first high point of the year; Easter was the second high point, the second great feast.

Sabina's father was a very generous man who raised his children to help each other. If someone in the family was sick, the others ran to help. If children needed to be minded, there was always someone there. If the field needed to be plowed, there was

Margaret at
age three

someone to do it. They were a family with tremendous faith and love.

Margaret at
Christmas-time

Although Sabina wanted to be a nurse, there was no money for nursing school. Instead, she studied accounting, went to work and never complained. At 24, she married a teacher and soon gave birth to two children. To them she gave her love of learning, education and music, especially Beethoven's Sonatas.

When her daughter Margaret went away to college, she encouraged her to stay true to her dreams. Although her father was not happy to see his daughter leave home, Sabina wanted Margaret to find her own path. Raising her children with a great sense of trust and support, Sabina always allowed them to make their own decisions.

And yet Margaret remembers that when she would leave for her dorm, her mother was always there at the bus station. As they would exchange parting words, Sabina would slip extra money into her daughter's pocket, followed by an extra embrace.

Margaret's College ID

At 21, Margaret decided to come to the United States. Again her mother trusted and supported her decision. Over family objections, she encouraged her. She supported Margaret. Sabina wanted her daughter to make not just a new life for herself but her own life.

Margaret remembers that her first days here were strange and sometimes overwhelming. Although she had family in the United States, she had left behind the most important person in her life, her mother.

She left behind the person who still helps everyone who needs assistance. She left the home whose door is still open to all. She left behind a woman who is a mama to her entire family of nephews, nieces, grandnephews and grandnieces.

And Margaret told me something else about her mother.

In fact, it is one of the most beautiful things I've ever heard about a mama. For Margaret, her basis for surviving in the United States was sustained by the memories of her happy childhood with Sabina. Her mama's love became the source of her strength. Her mama's love became her power base and Margaret says she can feel the love, even now, across the sea.

Margaret married my friend Gabe and Sabina has a grandchild, Zoe. She has made two trips to the United States to see them. So now even Zoe feels that special love from across the sea.

Margaret and Gabe

POLAND

Poland is a land of castles and skyscrapers. Mongols, Prussians, Germans and Russians have attacked Poland but the Poles have maintained a strong, national identity. Their music, dance, architecture, literature and science have influenced and changed world civilization. Their spirit, their faith has never been crushed.

In Poland, the past, the present and the future are intertwined. History occurs daily and is celebrated in actions and words. History is found in the stories that we tell. It is found in our shared history. And we summarize the lessons of our lives in words and phrases, always punctuated with "Mama says."

These three phrases are passed from
generation to generation...

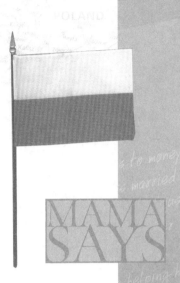

"What you don't learn, you will not know."

"The roots of learning are bitter but the fruit is sweet."

"You live and learn or you learn nothing."

This is the Polish way of saying what Mama
Lucia said in Argentina...

"What you do for God is what God does for you."

This phrase belongs to all people...

"Do not do anything to another person that you would not want done to yourself."

Each of us has a limit...

"A pitcher will carry water until its handle breaks."

Here is a Polish version of look before you leap...

"The farther you go into the forest the more trees you'll find."

Zoe and Grandma at her First Communion

And this is a great definition of hospitality...

"When there's a guest in the house, God is at home."

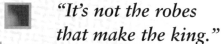

This intricate, handcarved wood box is an example of Polish folk art.

Every society has this one..

"The apple does not fall far from the tree."

"Don't teach a priest how to pray."

"It's not the robes that make the king."

50

Another way of "Too Many Cooks"...

"If there are six cooks in the kitchen, there will be nothing to eat."

Whenever the need occurs to buy something useless,

think of these words...

"As necessary as a hole in a bridge."

I love the Eastern European wolves...

"Invite a wolf for supper and you won't be around for breakfast."

Stefan Batory, the first king of Poland.

"When a wolf is chasing you, throw him a biscuit but don't stop to bake him a cake."

This quote is shared by the Poles and the Czechs.

I once heard President Havel of the Czech

Republic end a press conference with this saying...

"Never underestimate human stupidity."

Blessed Stanislaus who answers prayers.

"Better a helping hand than 100 pieces of advice."

Vittoria Maria Morandi

Nonna and Grandson Louis

This mama is my husband Lou's grandmother, Nonna, as he calls her. She was the most important person in his life, the person who gave him love and stability. Her house in Hazleton, Pennsylvania was home. She worked hard and never complained.

Her kitchen was always full of food and conversation; Sunday dinner at her house was the place to be. Every main course was accompanied by polenta and piverata and gnocchi, which she made using an old washboard.

Nonna always had at least two dogs and cats in the house. The animals never talked back to her and always ate everything she cooked for them, unlike certain fussy humans.

Nonna's Garden

Nonna Vittoria was a self-made woman. She scrubbed floors at Leo's Cafe and kept boarders, chickens, and even an ostrich. Her garden was her love, her work of art.

Lou always watched her and asked questions. She took him with her everywhere. When John F. Kennedy came to Hazleton, she was there, with grandchild in hand, to cheer the President as he passed through the streets.

She taught Lou to create and the first lessons were taught in Nonna's garden. It was she who gave him the basics and the skills to carve out his artistic talents. It was Nonna Vittoria, his mother, and his aunt who brought Lou to the Hazleton Art League for his first formal drawing lesson. Money was scarce but she believed in him. At the age of eight, he won prizes for both art and penmanship.

I recently began researching ancestors and I found that Vittoria Maria Morandi arrived at Ellis Island on July 15, 1923. Her age was 23. The information on the New York manifest is priceless. The questions she was asked and her responses to them show a truly strong-willed woman.

She made the trip to America alone, and she wanted the Ellis Island authorities to know that she paid for the trip herself. Her reason for emigrating was to join her husband in Walsemburg, Colorado. Neither a polygamist nor an anarchist, she intended to become a citizen and stay here always.

And stay she did. She gave birth to two daughters, Anna and Ida. She provided them with the education that would lead them to positions of professional and civic leadership in Hazleton. She lived to see them both honored as Hazleton's "Woman of the Year."

When she died, she left few material possessions. We have her crucifix, her sewing kit and some pictures.

One day I was sorting through these pictures when I found a small black diary. The book opened, on its own, to a page where Nonna had listed "Luigi Cannizzaro partito ai 13 agosto per New York. Venuto in casa 13 settembre 1959." That night, I showed Lou the page and I translated the words. "Louis Cannizzaro left for New York on August 13, 1965. He came into my home on September 13, 1959."

Nonna, Baby Lou, Aunt Ida and Mama Anna

We leafed through the book. Nonna's notations were few and terse. There were grocery lists, addresses, telephone numbers. Birthdays were listed and so too were dates marked with crosses, signifying the deaths of relatives in Italy.

Nonna's generation did not talk or brag about themselves. They were not into wasting time or describing events in flowery terms. They did not need to impress anyone or be impressed by anyone.

In her life, she had not accrued any financial wealth. What she had and what she had given could not be measured in terms of money.

Nonna's buttons from her sewing kit

Vittoria Maria Morandi had come to a new country and made it her home. She raised two daughters. She worked hard and expected everyone else to work hard, too. And she had a grandson whom she loved more than anyone or anything.

The only personal comments in the battered little book concerned her grandson. Lou lived with her for six years. He had come at age 4, a child of divorce, and left at 10 when his mother remarried. Although he visited her often, he would never again live with his grandmother.

She would never forget those years. She never told her cousins, her daughter, or her grandson about them. The time she spent with him was so important to Nonna Vittoria that she recorded them in the only valuable thing she owned, the book that was her most personal possession, her diary.

Lou and I both grew silent. We read the words again. They were simple words, almost totally monosyllabic. They were simple phrases with no adjectives or adverbs to cloud the facts and yet they were the most significant dates of her life.

"Louis Cannizzaro left for New York on August 13, 1965. He came into my home on September 13, 1959." With just a few words, his grandmother had told him how much she loved him.

Nonna's Diary entry

TRENTINO-ALTO ADIGE

The people from this region of Italy are the people of the

Nonna's Prayer Book

mountains, the Alps to the west and the Dolomites to the east. In fact, they were not made part of Italy until 1918.

In Trentino, they speak Italian. In Alto Adige, they speak German, Italian and their own language, Ladino. Once, their main city was Innsbruck and the proper name for their area is Sudtirol.

The Tirolesi know that the Alps and the Dolomites are filled with spirits that predate even Hannibal and his pachyderms. Nonna used to tell her grandson stories of devils and angels that inhabited her mountains.

She came from Bolzano, a place of castles, some still called by the German word "schloss." It was the place where Germans, Austrians, Napoleonic supporters and even Italians met.

When Nonna immigrated to the United States, she came first to Colorado and then to Pennsylvania. She had been born in the mountains and she chose to live and to die surrounded by mountains. And, here, she brought her stories, her legends and her words.

Nonna's life was guided by her Rosary. It traveled with her from Italy and traveled with her day by day. It remained her single most prized possession.

I can just hear Nonna announcing this one to the

Ellis Island authorities...

"Who doesn't want me doesn't deserve me."

Lou once asked her why she had come

to America and she said...

"If you risk nothing, you'll get nothing."

Another prized possession of Nonna's was her Grammar Book from her school days. She brought this with her to America and always kept it in a safe place all her life.

Here are two Italian versions of

"out of sight, out of mind"...

"Water that's far away won't put out the fire."

"If the eye doesn't see it, the heart won't desire it."

Prayer Cards of friends and relatives that bookmarked her Bible.

A Northern Italian definition

of friendship...

"When things happen, you'll know who your friends are."

Nonna must have lived this
because she was the first person
consulted when problems arose...

"Better a helping hand than 100 pieces of advice."

Nonna was a very resourceful person. Necessity is the mother of invention. When the handle of this vanity mirror broke, she crudely fixed it with a piece of hand carved wood and a few nails.
This too, was a possession from the "Old Country" as she so regularly referred to the mountains of her homeland.

Some things are just instinctive...

"You can't teach a fish how to swim."

And some things are just self-evident...

"Every pan has its cover."

One of Nonna's household hints...

"You can't have too many children or too many sheets."

And she firmly believed...

"If you give to receive, you'll get nothing in return."

Nonna was a seamstress. She saved the money she earned to buy a sewing machine to make clothes and curtains. The machine was in the kitchen where discussions on life and politics were always lively.

Grandma Anna Jane always said,
"God don't like an ugly."

Chicago • Via Mississippi

Fruteland Jackson

Fruteland Jackson, Bluesman, lecturer, storyteller
and author is to the Blues what Woody Guthrie
is to folk music. Performing solo and dedicated to
preserving acoustic Blues, Fruteland has been honored
with the Illinois Arts Council Folk/Ethnic Heritage
Award and the W. C. Handy Award for the Blues in
the Schools Education Program.

Fruteland considers himself a Blues Activist and
performs all over the world in theaters, clubs, cabarets and
festivals. Closest to his heart, however, is his "Blues in the
Schools" project for all children--the gifted, the high-risk
and those otherwise challenged.

When I first approached Fruteland about
this book, he responded immediately
and gave me the best definition yet for
my endeavors:

Fruteland's "Blues in the Schools".

"It has been a wonderful experience,
these past few days going over many of the old sayings
for what we call "isms" in the family. Just when you think
you're all out of them, you think of more. Homespun
wisdom. Words to live by, invisible cultural mechanisms
designed to live with you until you perish."

61

*Grandma
Anna Jane*

We corresponded and put together the following profile of two extraordinary women, Anna Jane Bradley and Ida B. Collins. They are, respectively, his maternal grandmother and his mother, and best described in Fruteland's own words.

My grandmother, Anna Jane Bradley, was born in Florence, Mississippi on January 10, 1908. She spent most of her life in a town called Doddsville. Born forty years after "surrender," the end of the Civil War, and about 55 years before the Civil Rights Movement, she resided in one house for over 70 years.

Her own mother and father had been forced to leave Florence. It seems that my great-grandmother was very beautiful and attracted much attention from the local male population. And, sometimes, she appreciated and reciprocated that attention. One night, both great-grandmother and great-grandfather were pulled from their beds, beaten in their front yard and told to leave. They settled in Ruleville, in the Mississippi Delta.

Grandmother Anna Jane worked in the home of a prominent United States Senator. Because she could pass for white, she traveled with the Senator's daughter. This relationship benefitted her social standing in the community.

Grandmother married five times. From her marriage to Sonny Collins, who was one-half Choctaw, a daughter was born, Ida B. This was my mother, born on February 18, 1926 in Doddsville.

Ida B. was able to attend college at Alcorn State. She lived on the "white folks" side of town, unlike her first cousin, Flora, who lived among the sharecroppers.

Mama Ida B. Collins and her parents

After World War II, mother married John Charles Chandler. The family grew to include six children. I was born in 1953 in Sunflower County, Mississippi and my grandmother predicted that "This gran'son is gon' be a preacha' and save souls."

Papa John and Mama Ida

My father was determined to escape farming and we went north to Chicago. He became an insurance underwriter and Mama became a licensed nurse at Chicago's Cook County Hospital. Through them, I learned about the cottonfields and Jim Crow. My mother died at a relatively young age and my grandmother's influence in our lives was to take on a more central role.

She was a Christian and a testimony to her life's work was the establishment of the New Jericho Missionary Baptist Church, located in Doddsville. Her name and the name of her last husband, Mr. Willie Bradley, are inscribed in the cornerstone.

A year before she died, I sang for her, a woman who detested the Blues. She pronounced it "Devil Music." I understood why she was uncomfortable. A lot of Blues songs are laid across old

63

church tunes. These songs are about drinking and women and sinning. But, I know, too, she was quietly proud of me.

Anna Jane's 50th Wedding Anniversary

Anna Jane Bradley died in 1998 at the age of 90. "Amazing Grace" and "Precious Lord" were sung at her church, the one with her name on the cornerstone. It was up to me, her grandson, to sing "When the Pearly Gates Unfurl."

That afternoon I sang the hymn again. I sang it at the Clarksdale Sunflower River Blues and Gospel Festival. I sang it for my grandmother Anna Jane, and I dedicated it to her.

Her words, long ago, had been realized. With my guitar in hand, I had found my pulpit.

My mother was gone. My grandmother was gone. Our history, our oral traditions and our music remain. For me, the Blues is the recognition of a tragedy and the optimism to deal with it.

I have lived in two worlds. I have lived in Chicago, in the North, the world my mother and father gave me. I have lived in Mississippi, in my grandmother's world, a place where I still feel a love-hate relationship.

Bridging these two worlds are the words of my mother and my grandmother. They have accompanied me for fifty years now, and they play as well as they read.

Grandmother Anna Jane on the human condition...

*"You can turn a mule
into a thoroughbred."*

*"You don't miss
what you
don't measure."*

"If you lie, you will steal."

*"Never take a shirt from
a naked man."*

*"Talking to you is like
singing a love song
to a hog."*

*Some of the tools of
the trade for a
bluesman and
storyteller*

65

The definition of a hard day's labor...

"To work from can see to can see."
(to work from sun to sun)

Beware the results of your actions...

"Bullets don't have eyes."

You don't need eyes to find your way...

"The palm can always follow the vine."

Grandmother and Mama on the subject of men and women...

"If you find a woman sitting on her front porch, leave her there."

"If you can't watch a woman 24 hours, don't try to watch her for 23."

"A woman knows what a woman needs."

More from Grandmother and

Mama on men and women...

"A man spends his time where he spends his money."

"Mama's baby, poppa's maybe."

"It is better to be loved than to be in love."

And Grandmother and Mama on religion...

"It is better to live in hope than to die in despair."

Grandma's Prayer Book.

"We must watch as well as pray."

And, my personal favorite...

"God don't like an ugly."

67

"The eyes are the mirror of the soul."

Sarah Ader

Sarah is one of my dearest friends. She came into my life at a time when I had convinced myself that my life was over. She, however, did not see it that way.

I had reached a crossroad. The road I had followed for almost 20 years was teaching. That road no longer held anything for me. Tossing aside security and all that was familiar to me, I decided to find a new path.

Sarah at my wedding reception

My family never understood my decision. Although my parents never spoke of it to me, I could see the hurt in their eyes. For them, a teacher was an object of respect. At home, I could feel their silent disapproval.

Sarah in Florida

I needed a new life. In the space of four years, Death had taken four people who had been at the center of my universe. I needed a new path. Finding one, however, was a bit of a trial.

One of the retired teachers from my former school, Red Spiliotis, had opened a travel agency. She needed help and I needed a job. What would be made quite evident in the following months was that Red was gravely ill. She was dying.

There, in Red's travel agency, in Park Ridge, New Jersey, is where I met Sarah Ader. She taught me a bit about the travel industry and a great deal about living life.

I had taken one year of sabbatical leave, without pay, from my former school district. In that year, my colleagues called and stayed in touch, supposedly awaiting my return. When I decided to leave teaching, the phone stopped ringing. Cobwebs grew along the telephone lines. My bitterness was manifest to everyone, except Sarah.

It was she who invited me into her home and family. She got me to take chances. She brought me into social groups and self-help groups. With every new step I took, she was by my side. No matter how large or small the step, she encouraged me.

We have worked together. We have been unemployed together. We have shared weddings and funerals and births and rebirths. We have commiserated over old memories and made new ones.

And it was Sarah who translated my "Something, something keppela" mystery. Years before, Pauline and Davey had prayed for blessings on my little head. Now, in Sarah, I have a blessing. I love her as my friend.

Words of wisdom come from many sources. They come from synagogues and shtetls. They come from thousands of years of wandering, from experiences both good and bad.

They come from oral history, from mothers to children.

Baby Jessica

The following sayings are now being passed to the fourth generation: from European grandmas to Sarah, to Cliff and Sharon, and to baby Jessica. In this family, they began with Sarah's second grandmother; her own grandmother had died in childbirth. When her grandfather remarried, the second grandmother was no wicked stepmother. She was a blessing, an angel to the entire family.

And Sarah Ader has been a blessing in my life. She pushed me into taking responsibility for my actions and helped me find a new way. It was the same old world but Sarah gave me new eyes with which to see it.

She has been there for me when I needed someone.
She still is. Mamas come in all forms.

Harold, Lou, Maria and Sarah

71

NEW YORK

There is no city in the world that represents the mixture of races, religions and cultures like New York. At one time, the lower east side was the center of Jewish life in the United States.

Tenements gave way to neighborhoods. Each street had its own style of living, its own rules. Identities were set, a blend of the Old World and a tough New World reality.

And when we speak of traditions and wisdom, the Jewish people have had thousands of years to gather their proverbs and sayings. May these words be preserved for thousands of years to come.

Each time I tell Sarah that something wonderful is about to happen, she says...

"From your mouth to G-d's ears."*

When there's disappointment, Sarah observes that...

"Man plans and G-d laughs."*

This one belongs to all people...

"One hand washes the other."

The old nuns used to say this, too...

"The eyes are the mirror of the soul."

72

Later, we worked in another agency in Westwood.

Whenever things appeared to be going too well, she would note...

"Never sing before noon. If you're too happy early in the day, you will cry the rest of the day.",

And this phrase usually accompanied the previous one...

"Never laugh too much because then you could end up crying too much."

I have been known to analyze something 6,000

ways and still not come up with a solution. After

much discussion and analysis, Sarah would always

solve the problem with this response...

"Don't think too much: G-d* will lead the way."

*In Orthodox Judaism, the Name of the Supreme Being cannot be taken for granted. It is not something to be lightly called upon or scribbled. Therefore, when the Orthodox write the word God, a dash is placed between the "G" and the "d" to prevent it from being defiled.

"Trust in God and be true to yourself."

Donald J. Trump

For me, New York will always be my home. I wanted
a special voice to represent my city. I wanted a person who
is known everywhere. I thought of Mr. Donald Trump.

He does not know me. We have never met yet he graciously
responded because that's what New Yorkers do.

I asked him about his mother's influence. I asked him if he has
key words to share, words that have sustained him throughout
his life. We went back and forth on the meaning of the topic
and, then, we found common ground.

When we delve into the depths of who we are, we find our mothers'
words. We come to realize how much we use their words and their
advice everyday. They carry us through and make us who we are,

"My mother would say,

"Trust in God and be true to yourself."

When I look back, that was great advice, concise and wise at
once. I didn't really get it at first, but because it sounded good
I stuck to it. Later on I realized how comprehensive this advice
was--how to keep your bases covered while thinking about
the big picture at the same time. It's good advice no matter
what your business or lifestyle, and has had a great
influence on me."

Donald J. Trump

*"Surrounding yourself with dwarfs
doesn't make you a giant."*

Blossom Miller

I first met Bobbie and her husband Irwin almost
30 years ago when the Millers walked into my
classroom for a conference. I was their daughter's
sixth-grade teacher and by the time they left,
we had become family.

The family grew, and in addition to Bobbie and Irwin,
included their daughters Suzann and Marion and
Bobbie's parents, Grandma Bessie and Grandpa Julius.

Bobbie on her wedding day

My father, mother and brother became part of the family, too.

Irwin worked for Burlington Industries and my mother had
worked in the garment trade in New York City, so they bonded
immediately. Bobbie and my father were great storytellers and
they could keep you enthralled for hours. But it was my brother
who made the difference. He was never comfortable with crowds
of people or with strangers, but he loved Bobbie.
He even knew her name. She was "Bobbie" and
Irwin was "the man."

Although Bobbie's roots went back to Eastern Europe,
I always think of her as a New Yorker. There was a
lot of 1667 Lexington Avenue about her.

Maria and Bobbie

Bobbie's door was always open. She was my shoulder
to cry on and my support when I needed support.

Everyone needs someone who listens and Bobbie listened to all my tales of woe and romance.

As Ecclesiastes advises, "To everything, there is a season." We had our seasons of joy, sometimes sadness, and many good times. In fact, it was at Bobbie's table that I became convinced that we Italians must be the long lost tribe of Israel. Her house was open to all and she welcomed all. And there was always food.

We had feasts that began in the early afternoons and extended into the nights and mornings, always punctuated by great conversations and political and artistic battles. And holidays were special. Rosh Hashanah and Yom Kippur, Chanukah and Christmas, Passover and Easter, we observed them all.

Hypocrisy was not a part of Bobbie's vocabulary or her life. One Passover, I can still remember her telling off her supposedly religious relatives. They were upset that "The Ten Commandments" was playing on one television network in competition with "Jesus of Nazareth." With roast chicken in hand, which she plopped in front of them, she announced that since she knew all about Moses, she had tuned in to "Jesus of Nazareth" because she wanted to learn this story, too.

Bobbie's Menorah which is still used for the holidays.

We trekked to Little Italy for the feast of San Gennaro. During the last game of the World Cup, the year Italy won,

78

everyone was gathered at our house.
Bobbie was detained and I said that I
would bring her to the party at half-time.
The situation did not look good for Italy.
The opposing team was Germany and
there was gloom all through our house.

Irwin, Bobbie and Mama
in Little Italy

During the second half Italy began to score. Bobbie announced
that it was her arrival that changed the course of soccer history.
When the Italians won, we had to wait until after sundown to
call our Orthodox friends. That night we had a feast and in
every Italian and Jewish enclave in New York there was a
celebration. The next day, we went to Irwin's old neighborhood
in Brooklyn. Since he had grown up with Italians, this was the
perfect place to be.

Bobbie was a life-long diabetic and in poor health. She never
complained and used her sense of humor to chase away any
sadness that touched her. In joy and sorrow, Bobbie was always
first on the scene with support. She sent Irwin with chicken soup
when someone was ill, and was the first to congratulate me when
I earned my Master of Science degree.

Although Irwin was transferred to North Carolina, we never
lost touch. When my parents were dying, they came back to
see them, to bid farewell to their dear friends. A year later
I took my then future husband Lou to meet them.

79

When Bobbie's health deteriorated, she and Irwin came back to our area. Being an invalid, however, was not on her agenda. We went to movies, museums and shops, and we dined together. The first evening they came back to my house for dinner, I placed them at the head of the table. I could see tears in their eyes because they were in my parents' chairs and they missed them.

Grandson Joshua

Bobbie's diabetes led to amputation, yet we continued to enjoy life to the fullest. After all these years, she was still the person who listened to me. She did what my mother could not do. When she spoke and offered her opinions, her words were never tinged with criticism. To her, I was another daughter, her friend, her Maria, her "Mamela." And in her living room, alongside her family pictures, there was another photograph. It was a picture of Lou and me on our wedding day.

Grandson Jason

Bobbie was no cliché. She was the personification of generosity.

Her death was a lie. The medics would have us believe that she had a poor heart. Her bravery in the midst of emotional and physical adversities negates all medical conclusions.

Granddaughter Michelle

I am here to testify that Bobbie had a great heart and she shared it with us all. I miss her.

THE BRONX

One million people reside in the Bronx, one of the 5 boroughs of New York City.

Bobbie's father, Julius, was a Kosher butcher and her mother, Bessie, was a bookkeeper. Celebrating their faith, the door was always open to everyone. On holidays, Grandma Bessie brought in strangers to dine with them. The parameters of their apartment were framed with love, faith and generosity.

Bobbie was born in the Bronx and her heart was as big as the Bronx. These are her words.

This was Bobbie's favorite expression. When unable to counter any obnoxious argument, she still wished good things for the speaker...

"May you live and be well."

After any failure, whether big or small...

"As we live, so we learn."

Bobbie had no tolerance for people who could not make decisions...

"You can't sit on two horses with one behind."

Mama Says

And this proverb also belongs to all people...

"The truth is not always what we want to hear."

There's an Italian version of this one, somewhere...

"An enemy agrees with you; A friend gives you an argument."

This was Bobbie's version of crying over spilt milk...

"After the head has been cut off, don't waste time over the hair."

Learning and experiences can be summed up

in simple phrases...

These goblets and spice tray were handed down though Bobbie's family and were only used during the High Holy Days.

"Happiness is not a horse that can be harnessed."

"Each day learns from the one that preceded it; no day prepares us for the one to come."

In my research, I have also found this beauty

in Russia and Eastern Europe...

"In the kingdom of hope, there is no winter."

82

My mother had her own version of this one, too...

"What you don't see with your eyes, don't invent with your mouth."

Jews, like Italians, are big on destiny...

"If a man is meant to drown, he'll die in a thimbleful of water."

No house was complete without its decorative figurines, also known as tchotchkes.

This may be one of the greatest bits

of business philosophy ever...

"Surrounding yourself with dwarfs doesn't make you a giant."

This phrase is straight from Tevye's mouth...

"If the rich could hire someone to die for them, the poor would make a wonderful living."

Bobbie's water pitcher, part of her trousseau

I was once hospitalized and Bobbie and Irwin rushed to the emergency room. Everything was somber. It was Bobbie who broke the solemnity with laughter when she took one look at me and exclaimed...

"Your health comes first; you can die later."

*"To be born noble is luck and not a virtue,
but to be ignorant is a man-made fault."*

Nonna Maria Stabillini and Nonna Santina Poli

When my parents died, I held onto the people who knew them. We converse in Italian and to hear the language of my parents is like hearing them again.

Paola and Luciano Neve are two of these friends. I have known them for 30 years. And again, we are crossing into four generations. When their daughter Barbara was born, I knitted a blanket for her and now, Barbara has a four year old, Allison, who is also bilingual.

Nonna Maria and Paola and Nonna Santina

Paola's story, however, goes back to Turin, the chief industrial city of Italy. It's about two extraordinary women who made

history in their own quiet way.

Nonna, in Italian, means grandmother and Nonna Maria Stabillini and Nonna Santina Poli were dear friends. Nonna Maria is Paola's mother and Nonna Santina's daughter married Paola's brother.

Barbara and Allison

Nonna Maria was one of 13 children, 10 of whom lived. The last child was called Ultimo, which means "the last" in Italian. Nonna Maria's mother made certain that all of them received an education.

Her father was a socialist and one of the leaders of a revolt against the local rich landowners. Their demand was simple: decent wages for the workers.

Nonna Maria's Family

Nonna Maria and Nonna Santina never criticized anyone. They fiercely defended their children and kept their families together as Italy changed from an agricultural society to an industrial one. They also kept them together through World War II. Being mothers wasn't something that just happened to them. Being mothers brought with it a sense of duty that expressed itself in caring not just for the family but for all who came in contact with them.

Nonna Maria had seven children, five of whom lived. She often said that her husband was her eighth child. Although he did not make enough to support them because he gambled, Nonna Maria never denigrated her husband to her children or anyone else. She kept the family together. She was its focal point, its heart. When I asked Paola for stories about her mother and Nonna Santina, she said that they were the sort of women who did things and never talked about them. They did what they had to do for themselves, their families and God.

Paola, however, remembered that once her mother took her to

find some food. It was wartime and provisions were scarce. They managed to buy a sack of potatoes. As they were walking home, the sirens began to blow. Nonna Maria pushed Paola against a building and covered her with her own body. She threw the sack on her shoulders and just waited out the attack. When it was over, both mother and daughter saw that the potatoes had saved Nonna Maria's life just as she had saved Paola.

In the final days of World War II, the partisans were rounding up any fascists they could find and executing them on the spot. One day they arrived at Nonna Maria's apartment building. As she was the custodian, she accompanied them as they searched the place and dragged out one of her neighbors.

Paola and Barbara

Nonna Maria placed herself between the man and the guntoting partisans. She told them that this man was her friend. Although his politics did not agree with hers, he had hurt no one. She asked the partisans if they had ever hurt anyone. In silence, they left. Paola witnessed this and questioned her mother but Nonna Maria gave neither an answer nor an explanation.

Her favorite saying to her children was, "There's no sense in looking at what you left behind: it's gone." Months later, Paola, was helping her mother clean the bedroom. As she was sorting through her bureau, she came upon a box filled with perfumed soaps and a comb. They were wrapped in delicate paper and ribbons. In postwar Italy, destruction was everywhere.

The discovery of soaps and ribbons was like finding a treasure and rediscovering a world that no longer existed.

Paola asked her mother where the soaps came from and to whom they belonged. Nonna Maria answered that they had belonged to people who had escaped during the war. She used the word "escape" and said they were Jews. She gave them clothes and they gave her soaps and a comb. When Paola asked what happened to the people, Nonna's eyes filled with tears.

It took years for Paola to realize that her mother, her mama, had helped Jews escape from Turin. She placed herself and the family she loved in peril to do what she knew to be right.

She blew no horns. She made no front pages of the newspapers. She received neither medals nor honors.

Nonna Maria kept the box until she died, awaiting the return of people who had, momentarily, come into her life. They had been strangers. They had not been family and yet, she had risked all that she held dear. They never returned.

When Nonna Maria died, half of Turin attended the funeral. People spilled into the streets to pay their respects. Her own children did not know the extent of her goodness and they still don't. That's often the case with mamas.

PIEMONTE, EMILIA ROMAGNA AND VENETO

These Nonnas can trace their roots to three provinces.
Piemonte means at the foot of the mountains, and the mountains
are the Alps. Turin, the major industrial city of Italy, was the
birthplace of modern Italy. The Piemontesi have the distinction
of being "falsi e cortesi." This means they lie to you but are
polite while they are doing it.

Emilia Romagna is an ancient region. Its capital is
Bologna, "la grassa" or "the fat," due to its great cuisine.

The Veneto comprises three areas and its chief city is Venice.
Dubbed "la serenissima," Venice is the Queen of the Adriatic.

To find work, these Nonnas and their families moved
to Turin. Here, they preserved their traditions, their
dialects, and their words.

Nonna Maria was the head of her family...

"Who has the spoon in hand mixes as he likes."

The Duomo of Turin, site of the Holy Shroud

We Italians believe in destiny and luck...

"Who is born unlucky has rain on his ass even when he's sitting.

89

Sometimes there's no room for doubts...

**"On the street of maybe-maybe,
one never-never goes home."**

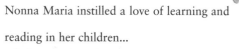

Nonna Maria did not take the
misfortunes of life seriously...

**"If the wise never made
mistakes, there'd be no
place for the ignorant."**

Nonna Maria instilled a love of learning and
reading in her children...

**"To be born noble is luck
and not a virtue,
but to be ignorant
is a man-made fault."**

Nonna Maria on children...

**"Small children give you a
headache; grown children give
you heartache."**

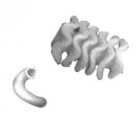

And here's one on friendship...

"He who trusts no one is trusted by no one."

My mama had a few like these...

"Trust few people and trust your relatives even less."

"Who waits for help from his relatives will wait until his teeth fall out."

This is the traditional bowl, la grolla, used for the communal imbibing of grappa.

In every cupboard in this area of Italy, a jar or tin of cornmeal for the making of polenta is always found.

This may be the best advice ever given by the Nonnas...

"If you want to be happy, look ahead and not behind."

"Even one person can make a difference."

Eleanor Burlingham

Years ago, when I made the decision to leave teaching, I found myself in economic peril. Working in a travel agency was not enough to compensate my former salary. My priest, Father Samuel Snodgrass, introduced me to Eleanor Burlingham, a true Boston Brahmin. 1667 Lexington Avenue met the Harvard Club. We liked each other immediately and I took on the role, if one can call it that, of Eleanor's administrative assistant.

Eleanor and my Mama in Eleanor's garden

Our relationship was often like a scene from "Driving Miss Daisy." Whether it was attending political rallies, attempting to boil maple syrup on her stove, or just driving through New England on holiday, it was a thrill to be with Eleanor. She was unique. Eleanor was game for everything. I even took her to her first McDonald's®. After ingesting her first and last Egg McMuffin® and hash browns, Eleanor remarked that all the food tasted the same and she did not know what all the fuss was about.

The Bethel in New Bedford

One summer, we decided to go on a *Moby Dick* odyssey. We stopped, first, as we always did in East Haddam and then progressed through New Bedford. We stayed at Melville House and explored the

93

Whaling Museum, the Seaman's Bethel and stood in the pulpit where Orson Welles delivers his sermon in the John Huston movie.

We headed to Aptuxcet to a small museum of artifacts. As an aside, Eleanor told me that it had been established by her Uncle Percival. We stopped in Gloucester

A Rock with Runes at Uncle Percival's Museum

to explore Our Lady of Voyage Church and the Sailor's Monument, "They that go down to the sea in ships." Our *Moby Dick* odyssey had turned into *Captains Courageous*. On our return, we stopped at Dartmouth College to see the Orozco Murals.

One summer we trekked to Maine to visit Eleanor's cousin, Naomi Burton Stone, who had been Thomas Merton's editor. Mentally equipped with a thousand questions, we found her still grieving over Merton's death. Good manners silenced all the questions. We proceeded to Rockland, Maine and the Farnsworth Museum where we consoled ourselves with the great paintings of N. C. and Andrew Wyeth.

Eleanor was a rarity, a person of principle. She could trace her lineage back to a Roman general named Fabianus. Her more recent relatives arrived in Massachusetts on the third ship to reach Plymouth Rock. She was born near the Harvard Club and an Anglican Bishop presided at her baptism. Armed with a law degree, she went to China with Owen Lattimore.

And yet the line that best describes Eleanor is from Kipling.
She could "walk with kings nor lose the common touch."
Always in a simple dress, poncho and sandals and always
carrying a small saddle bag, Eleanor faced the world with
her principles firmly in her heart. No matter what time of
year, the clothes remained the same. No matter what political
storms blew, her principles remained intact.

To be in her company was a learning experience. Her stories
were astounding. She had known writers, politicians,
statesmen, church men. She knew or had known everyone.

Eleanor loathed injustice and racism. She gave herself to causes,
both national and local, that she believed could make a change
in society. Several times she ran unsuccessfully for
Congress against a candidate who was an automatic
winner in our district. He would have run unopposed
but she believed that the people had a right to debate
and choose among differing opinions.

Eleanor had been born into Boston aristocracy
and could have been content with tea parties and
garden clubs. Yet, she always chose Robert Frost's
road, "the road less traveled." Many times, I saw
her stand up and espouse the political belief that
was not fashionable at that particular moment.
I saw her reduce many a gathering to silence.

RALLY
for
MICHAEL DUKAKIS
Democratic Candidate for President
and
ELEANOR BURLINGHAM
Democratic Candidate for Congress
and other Democratic candidates
PAUL O'DWYER
Democratic Elder Statesman
will be guest speaker
Come ! Discuss the Issues !

Refreshments will be served.
Donations will be welcome but are not required.
3:30 to 6:30   Sunday, October 23rd, 1988
At the VanderKloot Residence, 83 Ryerson Road, Warwick, NY

*Political Rally Poster
from 1988*

Once I asked her how all this had come to pass. In her rarified childhood, where did she first encounter injustice? She looked at me, softly called me "dear," because she always called me "dear," and told me about her mother.

Her earliest memory was of being taken to a rally in Copley Square. As she held tightly to her mother's hand, she glanced at the crowd. There were more people than she had ever seen. There were speakers, but she did not understand the words.

The crowd was silent, respectful of the speakers. Eleanor had never seen so many people gathered together. She had never experienced such silence. In a whisper, she asked her mother why they had come to this place. Her mother replied that they were there to protest the coming execution of two innocent men. I do not know if she had ever heard the words "protest" or "execution," but she knew the meaning of innocence. Then Eleanor asked who the men were. Her mother whispered the names Sacco and Vanzetti.

In the days to come, Eleanor's mother opened her home to Bartolomeo Vanzetti's sister. At her mother's side, Eleanor observed protests, appeals, demonstrations and the challenges that living in a free society entail. She never forgot the outrage and the sorrow that come when justice is denied.

We are what we are and our early influences are everything. As Wordsworth penned, "The child is the father of the man."

This also is true of women. It was from her mother that Eleanor learned about social injustice. She fought against it her entire life.

When she died, even her political opponents came to pay tribute. In 1992, in Rockland County, a park was dedicated in her memory. Since her death, the world and our nation have lived through terrible times. Very few people espouse or act upon principle. We are bombarded with the rhetoric of hate from newspapers, television and radio.
We shall survive.

Politics is a great deal like the fashion industry. Political theories, like the cut of clothes, go in and out of style, go in and out of vogue. Principles, however, are always timely. They never go out of style. Eleanor Burlingham lived what she believed and her beliefs were her life.

I cannot imagine her signing a document or swearing an oath or adhering to a dogma just because it is the safe thing to do, or the fashionable thing to do, or the flavor of the month.

Of all the people I have known, Eleanor Burlingham remains "A Woman for All Seasons."

ENGLAND

ENGLAND

Proud of her ancestry, Eleanor loved England's cathedrals, its green hills, and its literature. Her heart, however, belonged to its principles of government, its democratic traditions.

She was proud of Massachusetts and proud to be a member of the Democratic Party. There was a sense of fairness about her and she listened to all who came to her, seeking advice or help. She believed in democracy with a capital "D."

Eleanor's love of art and travel took us on many adventures. In Rockland, Maine we enjoyed the Wyeths at the Farnsworth Museum and the seafood at the Black Pearl.

Eleanor was known and respected in our small county. She was known and respected in the state of New York. And there are those in Washington, DC who still revere her. These are her words.

Eleanor was describing more than monetary remunerations when she said...

"A gentleman is known in the way he pays his debts."

The remains of New England's past shipping glory lie in Wiscasset, Maine.

Although she knew her campaigns were uphill battles, she believed her cause was just...

"You must make an attempt or you'll gain nothing."

I never saw her discouraged...

"The first blow fells not the tree."

"Who never climbed, never fell."

"One good turn deserves another."

This phrase could certainly apply to Eleanor, herself...

"Appearances are deceiving."

She surrounded herself with people from all walks
of life and she relished their company...

*"A man is known by
the company he keeps."*

*Eleanor's family had a home
in Gloucester and we
explored all the scenes from
Kipling's
Captains Courageous.*

She fervently believed in the importance
of conviction...

"Where there's a will, there's a way."

"It's never too late to live your life."

Eleanor's life was proof of this belief...

"Even one person can make a difference."

"You can't eat every bird that flies."

Alma Herman-Dzintars-Lemesis

In the early 1900's, Alma Herman-Dzintars-Lemesis was born in Latvia. The youngest of five, she was the granddaughter of Victor Herman, who lived to be 106 years of age.

For her, Latvia was a peaceful, bucolic country, a place where one could go berry picking without worrying about anything except the occasional wolf. And wolves figure greatly in Eastern European folklore.

Alma, today, still in charge of her life.

Latvia is Latvia, not Russia or Germany or Norway. Latvians speak Latvian, which dates to the time of Sanskrit. They have their own customs, arts and industries. Contrary to numerous claims of ownership, Latvians have always had their own identity.

Latvian Flag

When Alma's father was conscripted into the army, her mother, Eve, took the four children to Siberia. There, in the forest, she lived with her sister in a Latvian enclave. Eve survived the winters. Eve survived the wild animals.

One night, she even outwitted the human animals, robbers.

As they burned her cabin to the ground, she lowered her children one by one from the back window. With her own hands, she slaughtered the family pig to keep them all alive.

After Eve's husband returned from World War I, the refugees were allowed to return to their homeland. The trip was not first class on the Orient Express. They were crowded into animal cars and dysentery spread through the train. The Russian soldiers took the sick into the back wagon, where they were given "medicine." Only one person survived and he told the rest not to swallow.

Alma became sick and Eve hid her in a crate and, later, beneath her full skirts. Eve's husband and eldest daughter, however, both died and were buried in unmarked graves by the railroad tracks. At one point, the Russian soldiers herded everyone through one of the Czar's palaces. The idea was to show the Czar's corruption but Alma still recalls the beauty of the place.

Once home, they realized they had lost ownership of their family property. Eve was allowed use of the caretaker's cottage. All the children had to work but Alma wanted an education and attended night school. She had to walk to the school by crossing the Daugava River. She still remembers stepping from ice floe to ice floe in the cold northern waters.

As she tells it, Alma survived the German and Russian occupations of World War II with a dash of luck. She was married now with her own child. Once, she was in the closet when the soldiers came for her. Another time, she was unharmed after an air raid, shielding her baby.

As the Soviets began to close in, they got a fast horse. Then the family boarded a ship, the last one to get through safely. All their belongings are still buried in Latvia and somewhere hangs a meal in a well, awaiting their return.

Ilze, Eve and Lucas

Alma had another son much later in life and then the bonus baby, Ilze. This pregnancy almost brought about her death from gestational diabetes but she had her little girl. And, of course, the only girl was a tomboy.

Quietly fiercely independent, Ilze refused ribbons and dolls. She escaped into thunderstorms, ran along Iroquois deer paths and was twice downed by lightning. She spent her childhood in the wild, working with horses. She was as good a shot as the boys and learned to drive in a Corvette. She even played electric rock guitar.

When Ilze turned 16, she left her hometown, never to return. She was full of adventure as are all mothers. After all her travels and trials, Ilze has learned that there is nothing more precious on the face of this earth than her children, Eve and Lucas. There is no greater joy than the love she gives them and no greater strength than the joy they give her.

Lucas's Birthday

Ilze grew up listening to stories of love and survival, and she has a few of her own. Her fondest memory of her mother, Alma, is a night long ago. She was still a child. She was still part of her forgotten hometown.

It was winter, not a Russian winter but nonetheless, winter. Ilze and her mother walked miles into the forest. There are some who say that you can never be lost in a forest. It was upstate New York, not Latvia or Siberia.

Ilze wanted to bring hay and carrots and apples to the wild animals. It was cold and they needed her. Mother and child walked through the woods together. It was a special night. It was Christmas Eve. There are times in a person's life when there is no one — except God and mother.

Written by Ilze Lemesis and edited by Maria L. Valdemi

LATVIA

This land on the Baltic Sea was first settled in 10,000 B.C. The people known as the Balts, however, arrived in 2000 B.C. The Roman historian Tacitus wrote that the early Latvians were the people who lived on the Amber Sea.

From the thirteenth to the twentieth century, one foreign power or another has overrun Latvia, be it Livonian Knights, Swedes, Germans or Russians. The Latvian language, a key to their identity, is neither Slavic nor German. It is similar only to Lithuanian.

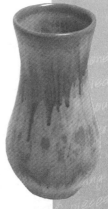

These are examples of Latvian folk art.

Almost half of Latvia is forestland. Legends and poems immortalize the inhabitants of these forests. There are wolves and werewolves and bears. In fact, the Latvian national poem is called "The Bear Slayer." There is even a castle where a maiden was killed and where she still appears by the light of the full moon.

Latvia is also a land of music where legends and poems are set to melodies and preserved from one generation to the next. An entire nation has been preserved in its own unique language and music. Here, then, are some of the sayings of Latvia.

This is a Latvian version of the old dog and new tricks...

"A dog sheds fur but a man cannot shed his habits."

This one reminds me of my mother and the onion...

"A smiling face is half the meal."

Mama Alma on happiness...

"You can't eat every bird that flies."

Mama Alma on the human condition...

"Once an ass, always an ass."

"A pig is always a pig."

Eastern Europe is renowned for its amber jewelry.

And in the same vein...

"If you marry a pig, don't be surprised when you give birth to piglets."

Here's the Latvian cart before the horse...

"Don't sell the bear until you've caught him."

"You cannot make a nightingale out of a crow."

And here's a wish for old age...

"Live a lifetime, learn a lifetime."

This is Mama Alma's

favorite saying...

" Don't borrow trouble — you have enough of your own."

And now for the wolves...

"A wolf has a wolf's nature."

A few pieces of Alma's remaining jewelry, passed down to Ilze.

This is my favorite...

If you're going to hang around with wolves, you'd better learn to howl.

An antique doll in native
Latvian costume

107

*"A book is a ship
that can take you far away."*

Edna Graham Wilson

Edna and Clyde Wilson, their daughter Carol, and their Boxer Suzy were one of the original families on our street. Clyde was one of the hardest-working men I've ever known.

Without complaint, every morning he left for work in New York City. And every evening he returned, had his dinner, and relaxed in his living room beneath a picture of the Delaware Water Gap.

Edna's daughter, Carol, on her wedding day

Mrs. Wilson stayed home. Crippled with arthritis, her hands were bent and she walked slowly. I saw her cry with pain yet I never heard her complain. And I never heard Mr. Wilson bemoan his fate in life. In an ordinary place in the world, these were two extraordinary people.

My mother and Mrs. Wilson shared an ethnic bond. They were both New Englanders. Mama was born in Pittsfield, Massachusetts and Mrs. Wilson was born in Providence, Rhode Island. Proud of Roger Williams, religious tolerance and the fact that her state had been the first to declare slavery illegal, she believed Rhode Island to be the greatest state in the Union. The two women were soon inseparable.

Rhode Island Flag

We went food shopping once a week. At that time there was only one store, the Grand Union in Haverstraw.

My mother would place my brother in the child's seat of the cart. Mrs. Wilson would follow behind with her cart. It did not take long for the five-year-old me to see that people were staring as we passed through the aisles.

They were staring at my brother, my retarded brother, always child like. Yes, I use the word retarded because that was the word in the 1950's. They were staring at Mrs. Wilson, too. I, of course, took this all personally.

I didn't hesitate to act. Whenever I saw someone staring or laughing, I'd fly right over to them. Clenching little fists, I would ask what they were staring at, what they wanted. I never got a response but that didn't stop me. I would then ask if they wanted a picture because I could get one.

Mama did not approve of such behavior. She devised a plan, a diversion. I was learning to read, devouring anything in sight, and she promised me a Golden Book if I was a good girl. In those days Golden Books, a series of children's stories, were displayed at the front of stores.

If memory serves me well, the plan was not a success. I next remember being parked at the Grand Union's entrance where I leafed through several Golden Books while they shopped.

New England

When Mama and Mrs. Wilson were ready to check out,
Mama would return for me and let me select a book.

One day, I saw tears in Mrs. Wilson's eyes. As we were leaving
the store, my mother turned to her fellow New Englander. In her
way of saying "Consider the Source," my mother told us that
stupid things are said by stupid people. Therefore, we should
not concern ourselves with the stupid ravings of stupid people.

Edna Wilson was a voracious reader, something we
had in common. Sometimes my mother would send
me over to the Wilson's with something or for
something. In the 1950's, women borrowed an egg
or a cup of flour or a cup of milk when they ran short
for their recipes. After awhile I did not need a pretext.

The Wilson's house

In the Wilson's cellar, there was an upright piano. I would open
the top and climb into it and place myself among some rather large
books. With a child's eye and mind I perused them and tried to
make sense of the stories and poems.

One rainy day, I opened one of the volumes. It fell from my
hands and caught in my lap. The left side held words arranged
in such a way that I knew it was poetry even if I could not
understand all the words.

My eyes glanced at the right side, to a black and white
reproduction of a painting. It was love at first sight.

111

Even now I can still feel the joy I experienced over half a century ago. The picture had a title, Sir Galahad, and below it were the words: "My strength is as the strength of ten because my heart is pure."

I do not know how many minutes or hours I gazed at Sir Galahad. With tome in hand, I do remember running up the stairs and asking Mrs. Wilson to explain the picture. And she did.

With stories in my head, I began to visit the Stony Point Library. I would bring a bag to carry all the books home. If I could not get a ride I would walk there. Mrs. Wilson and I both had cards and I would select books for her. She loved mysteries.

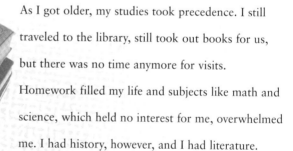

As I got older, my studies took precedence. I still traveled to the library, still took out books for us, but there was no time anymore for visits. Homework filled my life and subjects like math and science, which held no interest for me, overwhelmed me. I had history, however, and I had literature.

One adolescent summer, I discovered Emily Brontë and *Wuthering Heights*. It so happened that the revival of the 1939 movie masterpiece was making the rounds. Mama was now driving. After much pleading, we ventured to Cinema 45 in Spring Valley to see the Olivier-Oberon interpretation. As we approached the parking lot, we saw that the line of people waiting to see the movie extended into the street.

Undaunted, we took our places: Mama, my brother, Mrs. Wilson and I. We could not get four seats together. Mrs. Wilson and I found seats in the middle of the last row. It was hard for her to maneuver over those legs and feet but she did it.

The lights went out and the opening credits appeared. The music surged and silence overtook us, soon replaced by awe. By the time we reached Olivier's classic, "I cannot live without my life, I cannot die without my soul," we were both crying.

The Wilsons retired to Florida. Mrs. Wilson did not want to leave my mother. With their departure, one part of my life was over.

Half a century has passed since we moved to Stony Point. Sometimes I feel the years and sometimes I feel like the child who discovered Sir Galahad, one rainy day in memory.

The same poet, Tennyson, who wrote the words beneath the black and white reproduction, wrote the words that have served my life: "Much have I seen and known, I am a part of all that I have met."

Through Edna Wilson's example, I learned that a body can be physically limited, but the places and the spaces a mind can reach are infinite. Her spirit lives in her daughter, her grandchildren, Joseph and Michael, and her great-grandchildren.

And she lives in me for I love mysteries. I, too, love books. May such a spirit be part of every child's life.

NEW ENGLAND

Edna Graham Wilson was a Rhode Islander by birth who could trace her family to Scotland. She could quote both Shakespeare and Robert Burns and spoke with a New England accent.

The Cross of St. Andrew, Scotland

She loved Tartan plaids and fish and chips. She loved nothing better than a cup of tea in the afternoon and good conversation.

The beauty of a language is not just in its writings. A language is preserved only when it is spoken. I was fortunate. An expert read the first great works of English literature to me. She was a Rhode Islander by way of Scotland. And these are her words.

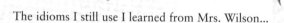

The idioms I still use I learned from Mrs. Wilson...

"As sweet as maple syrup."

"As big as a moose."

"As thin as a rail."

"As dull as dishwater."

"As right as rain."

"A watched pot never boils."

114

Whenever I voiced my childhood complaints,

she would say...

"Time heals all wounds."

MAMA SAYS

Mrs. Wilson used to say to me all the time...

"A book is a ship that can take you far away."

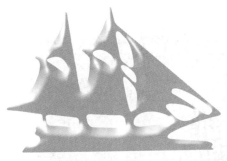

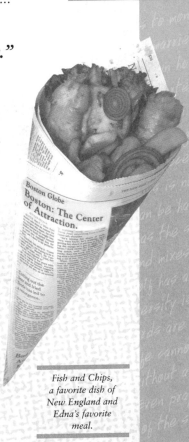

And, this is so like a New Englander...

"If you want to listen, close your mouth."

And, like my Mama, she believed...

"There is no life without hope."

Fish and Chips, a favorite dish of New England and Edna's favorite meal.

"Blessed is he who expects little.
He is seldom disappointed."

Tony Hillerman

When we returned from our visit with R.C. Gorman, a
message was waiting from the great writer, Tony Hillerman.
He is my favorite novelist and an award-winning mystery
writer. I knew that, somewhere, Mrs. Wilson was smiling.

Dear Maria Valdemi:

Alas, I was doing those publication things in New York and
Washington while you were in New Mexico. Sorry I missed you.

My mother, Lucy Grove Hillerman, taught her three youngsters
a lot of things, but the one I guess affected my life the most was her
emphasis on courage. *"Blessed is he,"* she would tell us, *"who expects
little. He is seldom disappointed."*

I used that *"Seldom Disappointed"* as the title to my autobiography
partly because it has such a nice ironic ambiguity in it. For her it meant
more than merely lowering one's expectations to a reasonable level.
It meant don't take disappointments seriously. Forget them. Move on.
Be happy.

Perhaps more important, she taught us not to be afraid. *"You're born.
You live awhile. You die. Death is inevitable. Look at it. Get acquainted
with that truth. And don't waste the time you have worrying about
being hurt."*

Mama was an R.N., joined the Army in World War II and, needless
to say, got acquainted with death at close hand--not just the fallout
from battle but that terrible "black flu" epidemic which raged in
1917-19 and killed more people than the war.

As a teen-ager she and her brother had taken their horses and wagons
and headed into the big emptiness of the Oklahoma Panhandle to file
homestead claims, build a sod house, and live the required year to earn
title to the land. After that, after nursing school, after the War, she met
the man who would be my father--then a widowed father of two
daughters. That, too, demonstrates a high level of courage.

We were never ever taught to be afraid. Nothing mattered except
using that time between birth and death for the purpose God intended.
He gave us a conscience. Follow it. He taught us, through the gospels,
a moral code. Feed the poor, clothe the naked, visit the sick, never lie,
be ready for our merciful God to welcome us home for the last
great adventure.

Sincerely,

Tony Hillerman

*"Words are like sparrows.
When they fly out,
they cannot be retrieved."*

Marina P.

After my brother died, my mother returned to work, earning a salary outside the house. She had cared for her son for 28 years and without him, the house must have been a lonely place. My father was at work. I was at work. She was alone.

Mama found employment in a small factory in Haverstraw. There, she met Marina.

They began exchanging recipes and stories and, soon, our families were sharing dinners. I went along because one of my majors in school was Russian History and I love Russian Art and Literature.

We sat for hours discussing poetry and opera and history. Marina was from Leningrad but her husband, Stefan, was born and raised in the countryside.

Matrushka means little mother and this nesting doll is a symbol of Russia.

An old believer, he had practiced his religious faith secretly in the woods and in the forests.

Through famine, purges and politics, the Russians kept their beliefs. Great books were banned. Like something out of *Fahrenheit 451*, people set their favorite poems to music and passed them on to their children so the words and the poets would never be forgotten.

119

We would speak of Tsetayeva and Akhmatova and Yesenin.
Marina, naturally, loved Marina Tsetayeva, a poet who was
tricked by Stalin's agents into returning to Russia. There, her
husband and son were killed. In despair, she took her own life.

Anna Akhmatova, my favorite and one of the greatest poets
of any country, lived through the 900 Day Siege of Leningrad.
She even survived a Stalinist prison camp to write of her
sufferings, of her people. Stefan loved Sergei Yesenin.
He was the peasant poet, the last poet of the countryside.

Marina and Stefan took me to their Russian Easter Service.
It was astounding—the music, the incense, the candles—
a truly awesome experience. Afterwards, the entire congregation,
including me, proceeded to the Church Hall for a goose dinner
with all the trimmings.

We had fun. I remember one icy Saturday morning. Our region
had been hit with a storm and all were advised to stay off the
roads. A lone car inched its way up our street and out stepped
Marina. She announced that we were going for a ride—
and we did.

What a ride! Stefan drove that car like a troika, a Russian sled.
We slid over the roads and into the woods of Harriman State Park.
The trees were encased with ice, glittering like diamonds.
The sun danced through the ice crystals, forming prisms of color

that shone like jeweled rainbows. It was the Kingdom of the
Snow Queen and we were her official courtiers.

At Christmas time I took Marina to New York. One of the
theaters was showcasing Russian ballet movies and I offered
her a ticket for this show as a Christmas present. Stefan
did not want to attend the ballet, even a movie version. I gave
him a picture of Sergei Yesenin instead and he was very happy.

I do not remember the movie. I do not remember the ballet,
at all. I do remember that after we left the movie, we walked
toward 57th Street to the old Russian Tea Room. It was
between curtain times and there were tables available.
I convinced Marina that we could have a light snack.

The Russian Tea Room was always decorated for Christmas.
The lights were encircled with golden garlands and Christmas
ornaments. The place was always set for a celebration.

As we talked, I saw that Marina's
exuberance had waned. I thought that
I had made a mistake bringing her to
the restaurant. Perhaps it reminded
her of the Russia that she could
never have again. As my eyes reflected
the Christmas ornaments, I regretted
my spur-of-the-moment decision.

And then, Marina told me a story I shall never forget. Stefan was her second husband. She had met him in the prison camp. I said nothing.

When the Nazis invaded Russia, her first husband was called up for military duty. She took her daughter and went south of Leningrad to be with her mother. As the Nazis swept through, they killed those who were of no use to them and took prisoner those who could be forced into hard labor.

Marina, her mother, and her daughter were sent to a slave labor camp. Like animals, they wore yokes, carrying water, wood, cement or anything the guards told them to carry. To the Nazis, the Russians were subhuman, fit only to be beasts of burden. Marina asked me if I could imagine what that was like. My eyes looked up at the Christmas ornaments. I said nothing.

One day, Marina's mother realized that she could go no further. Each of us has our moment. Each of us will have our moment. Marina's mother put the yoke down and knelt upon the ground. The work line came to a stop. A guard started yelling. Marina's mother did not rise. The guard started to bludgeon her with his heavy staff. Still, she did not move.

Everything came to a standstill. Then other guards rushed over and they also began to beat the woman. With a yoke across her shoulders, Marina froze. She did not run to her mother's assistance. Before her eyes, she saw her mother beaten to death.

From across the table, Marina gazed at me. She asked me if I knew why she had not run to her mother. I said nothing but, in my mind, I thought that she had wanted to stay alive for her daughter.

With tears in her eyes, she took my hand. Had she run to save her mother, Marina's daughter would have run to help her. Fearing a riot, the guards would have fired their rifles. The one most likely to be shot was her daughter. My eyes filled with tears now, and not from the sight of Christmas ornaments.

After all these years, I can still hear her say, "I had to save my daughter." After all these years, I can still hear her asking me, asking me, if she had made the right decision.

We lost touch when Marina's daughter, husband and grandchildren were transferred to Europe. Her son-in-law's business brought them to London. Marina and Stefan went, too.

Her daughter wanted to be near her mother. Her daughter wanted her children to be with their grandmother.

I hope that was the answer to Marina's question to me.

Marina had watched her mother die. Marina had saved her daughter and that daughter, now, has children. And they carry the traits of some very brave people.

Once there was a rotten prison camp in what was then a rotten part of the world. In that place, a woman, surrounded by death, had chosen life.

She was a mother and that's what great mothers do. They choose life.

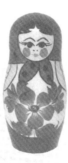

RUSSIA

It is said that Russia is a mystery wrapped in an enigma.

The Russian people have known great suffering. Millions have died at the hands of tyrants. Millions perished in both world wars. Their collective soul, however, survived in art, music, dance and literature. This soul is their identity. It is their real heritage.

Here there is neither mystery nor enigma. If you seek the heart of a people, read their sayings and listen to their words.

This was Marina's favorite saying…

"Judge by deeds, not by words."

My mama used to say this, too…

"Each seed knows its time."

"If you sit between two chairs, you'll fall."

The Easter Egg is one of Russia's most famous traditions.

"Not everyone who has a cowl is a monk."

This Fairy Tale box was a gift from Marina.

Here are those wolves again…

"Wolves don't eat wolves."

This is the Russian version of "Don't cut off your nose to spite your face"…

"Don't cut the branch you're sitting on."

The writer, Turgenev, expressed the same sentiment...

"Do not measure others by your own values."

This ceramic piece is a modern version of a traditional costume.

Here's a Russian version of Mrs. Wilson's saying...

"Words are like sparrows. When they fly out, they cannot be retrieved."

Marina on the human condition...

"If you knew where you'd fall, you'd spread some straw."

"Even prayer taxes the mind of the stupid."

"Eggs cannot teach a hen."

"You can't drink soup with a knife."

"A kind word is like a spring day."

A Russian way of saying there is always something to aim for...

"There is always a higher mountain."

And my personal favorite...

"Life cannot be endured without a dream."

*"All that glitters is not gold
and fools rush in
where angels fear to tread—
all for that gold!"*

Anne Keane Higgins

Let me begin this chapter by saying that I have been surrounded by Irish-Americans all my life. The nuns who were my teachers were, for the most part, Irish. Our parish priests were, for the most part, Irish. My schoolmates were, for the most part, Irish.

Anne in her youth.

And this all came about because my mother wanted her own house and garden. Had we stayed at 1667 Lexington Avenue, the incarnation of our Blessed Mother would have been Our Lady of Mt. Carmel and my school would have been St. Cecilia. However, we moved to Stony Point and the incarnation and the school became one, Immaculate Conception.

As John Lennon wrote "there are places I remember" but there are also people. It is easy to have a friend who tells you exactly what you wish to hear and agrees with your every word. It is a rare blessing to have a friend who tells you the truth. For the years I taught Middle School I had such a friend, Eileen McHugh.

Eileen

Her mother, Anne Keane, was born in 1906 in County Sligo. She was the youngest in a farming family and like so many before her, she emigrated to the United States. She lived with her sister, Mary and they both worked in the rectory of St. John's in Kingsbridge.

129

She met her husband, John Higgins, at a dance. They had known each other in Ireland but since she was three years older, nothing came of it. But here, in the New World, there was no age taboo and they were free to love.

Anne Keane's Wedding Day

They married in 1936 and all the guests were treated to a wedding breakfast. John Higgins went into the restaurant business, building and owning bars and grills, and even a nightclub. But in the beginning, there were just dreams. Their first apartment was on Briggs Avenue in the Fordham section of the Bronx.

Anne was first, born in 1937. She was followed by John in 1941 and Eileen in 1945. Nine months later, they bought a two-family house in Woodlawn. Although they had the opportunity to purchase a single-family house in Yonkers with more property, it was situated on a main thoroughfare and this Irish Mama did not want her children crossing back and forth over a highway.

The house in Woodlawn had another advantage, however. It was just half a block from the church and school, St. Barnabas. In this house, memories were made. Anne Higgins devoted her life to her family. In the mornings, there were hot breakfasts

Mama, Anne and Eileen

and in the winters, warmed underclothes and socks.

The three children came home every day for lunch. After school, there were snacks and treats and word spread that the Higgins house was the place to be for rest and recreation. She welcomed all to her home.

Anne Higgins loved to laugh. She took joy in her life. And at the end of the day she was never too tired to share a laugh or a story with her children. She was always there for her children.

Every day, winter or summer, Anne Higgins attended 6 A.M. Mass. She did not preach to her children. Her method of teaching was by doing, not by saying. She had an eighth-grade education but she could hold her own in any debate or discussion. She had an innate grace that cannot be taught, a charm that defined her. She was respected by all who knew her.

In 1952, John Higgins died. Anne believed she was not qualified to work outside the home so she rented out an apartment in her family house. This was her way of sustaining her family without uprooting them.

Grandma and Granddaughters at her favorite house

No one in the neighborhood knew of their plight for she never complained to anyone. She could make do with nothing, but her expectations for her children never changed.

All three went to college, but her youngest, Eileen, married a New York City policeman, Michael McHugh, in 1965. After two years of college, they decided to start a family. She found work as a part-time salesclerk. Michael, Jr. was born in 1966 and John was born in 1967.

Eileen and Michael

Anne watched the two children when Eileen went to work. She knew, however, that her youngest was meant to achieve more in life. One day she turned to her and said, "Eileen, do you intend to be a salesgirl all your life? When are you going to return to school and get your degree?"

My friend needed no further prodding. She returned to Mt. St. Vincent's and earned her Bachelor of Arts Degree in 1971. Then, she attended the College of New Rochelle. When Eileen received her Master's Degree, her mother knew her task was completed. All three children had gone to college and all three had attained advanced degrees.

And the years passed with Easter and Christmas dinners at the house in Woodlawn. For Christmas, there was prime rib roast with home-made gravy, her very special roast potatoes, perfectly crisp and Brandy Alexanders. For Easter, there was lamb and asparagus and ambrosia.

All holidays had trifle for dessert. Her recipe consisted of ladyfingers, fruit, Jell-O®, whipped cream; she added brandy for her son-in-law, Jerry.

There was a children's table, the chairs made by turning wastepaper baskets upside down and topping them with a pillow. They had been specially purchased to be chairs and were easily stored away until the next holiday.

The trifle bowl used for dessert was as much a tradition as the holiday itself.

She made the Easter Baskets and hid them. She delighted in her grandchildren. The family had grown to include Darby, Eileen and Michael's daughter. When asked why she had never returned to Ireland, Anne Higgins answered that her family was here.

In her later years, she was legally blind, yet no one knew it. She knew every inch of her home so well that she was able to maintain it on her own.

When Anne was diagnosed with congenital emphysema, the doctors recommended that she be placed in an assisted living residence. My friend Eileen told them that such an action would kill her mother. When she confronted the doctors, she says it was the proudest moment of her life. She had returned to her mother the gift she had given to all three of her children—life.

The McHughs when they came into my life

Anne Higgins stayed in her home until her death in 1992. In her eulogy, her eldest grandson, Michael, recalled all the Easter and Christmas dinners at that wonderful house in Woodlawn. Like the house she had maintained so well, she had loved and respected life with that same dignity.

*Eileen and Michael McHugh's
25th Wedding Anniversary*

Our time here is allotted to us. Sometimes, it is a short run. Other times, it is a long haul. What is important, however, is that which we leave behind. It may be places. It may be people. Anne Higgins came to a new country. She married and raised a family. She had a house that was not merely walls and furniture and acreage.

Anne Keane Higgins had a home.

IRELAND

Ireland, like Italy, is a nation that transcends its borders. The Irish are a hard working people whose nation was occupied. Although attempts were made to destroy the Irish, their faith became their means of survival.

When my mother returned to the United States in 1933, it was August the 2nd, just days before her thirteenth birthday. Her Uncle Sam's farm consisted of 350 acres. It was a lonely, cold place for a child who had known only the sun. The nearest neighbor was Pat Gibbon and his wife and three daughters.

The farm had no running water, no electricity. There
was no woman to serve as a comfort for a young girl.
That first night, my mother cried herself to sleep.

On August 4th, there was a knock on the door. Mrs. Gibbon and
her three daughters entered. In the midst of the depression, a lady
had found some flour, sugar and eggs to make a birthday cake
for a girl who had never had a cake or any sort of celebration
to mark her birth. My mother never forgot that act of kindness.
It would always be equated with an Irish lady.

We preserve the stories of our families with our words. In the
same way, we preserve the stories of our ancestors. With wit
and with love, I present the words of another Irish lady.

Like all the immigrants to our country, Anne believed...

"You make your own luck."

Anne's Teacups

Eileen remembers that her mother had no patience with fools...

"Here's your hat. What's your hurry?"

If she was invited somewhere and the food was not good, her response was…

"Thanks for the tea. The room was lovely."

The Celtic Cross is a symbol of Irish faith.

Her most important advice she reserved for her daughters. She wanted them to be able to make their own living…

"A woman must be independent."

"If you bring a whole and intact person to someone, then you're really bringing someone. You must be somebody."

"If you're complete with yourself, then you have something to give."

This is great advice concerning marriage...

"You can marry a rich man as well as a poor man."

"It takes pains to be beautiful— both outside and in."

"All that glitters is not gold and fools rush in where angels fear to tread— all for that gold!"

And, this was Anne Keane Higgins's

philosophy of life...

Anne's Rosary which has now become a family heirloom.

"As long as you've done your best, you've done well."

137

"Always do your best"

COLLEGE OF
MOUNT SAINT VINCENT

SISTER ELIZABETH MARIAN MURRAY

MEMORIAL LECTURE SERIES

Presents

Billy Collins

Thursday, February 13, 2003

8:00 P.M.
Smith Hall

Pamphlet for Billy Collins's
Lecture Series

Billy Collins

After many years of joys and sorrows, I called Eileen McHugh because I wanted her to be part of this book. The first night we were scheduled to meet, she called with a better idea.

Billy Collins, the Poet Laureate of the United States, was being hosted at her alma mater, Mount Saint Vincent. As part of the Sister Elizabeth Marian Murray Memorial Lecture Series, he would be reading his poems.

Of course I agreed to come. I hadn't done anything literary in years. I had been especially moved by the poem he had written as a memorial to the people of September 11th, 2001. It is the most beautiful tribute of all the words I have read.

After the lecture, he stayed at the college and we had a chance to meet with him. I boldly told him about my book and asked him for a quotation about his mother. He smiled and said that the most important thing she had ever impressed upon him was

"To always do your best".

I thanked him and I glanced at Eileen. I know that in that moment she had heard the voice of Anne Keane Higgins.

Billy Col

Mama Says

Afterword

My life has been influenced by people, places and events. I am grateful to all the teachers, to all the books, to all the great works of art that have influenced my small path.

And, for the most part, it has been a good trek. Yet Bertolt Brecht wrote that it isn't necessary to say that someone or something is good; rather, let it be said that you accomplished good and left the world a better place.

The foundation of all societies is the family. The heart of the family is best defined by the mother.

All the mothers I have written about are real people with all their joys and sorrows. As they raised their families, they endeavored to instill and to preserve their values and their experiences.

Their lives are not recorded in the annals of history. Their stories are not found in the immortal tracts of literature. Their portraits do not grace the hallowed walls of the great museums of art.

It seems a harsh judgment. Do we judge a mother by the number of offspring she produces? Do we judge a mother by her cooking skills? Do we judge a mother by the neatness of her house?

The mothers I have portrayed all had two traits in common. The first was unshakable faith, a faith they lived and exemplified in their everyday worlds. And the second trait has nothing to do with offspring, recipes or a clean house. This trait is love.

I remember a phrase written by another mother, Mother Teresa. She believed that in the final analysis, we will not be valued for all the real estate and property we leave behind. Judgment will be based on how we loved.

My mother, like all the women in my book, had a special love. And neither oceans nor continents nor death can separate me from that love.

When the peonies and the lilies bloom in her garden, I see my mother. When Easter returns, I feel her presence as I follow her faded recipe and bake her braided Calabrese bread. And when all the birthdays and the holidays come, I know she is by my side.

In those moments, I remember her love. And in the silence of my heart, I hear her words.

Acknowledgements

I want to thank all my friends and family beginning with Elizabeth Mondo, Yolanda Aramendi, Margaret Miglionico, my husband, Louis Cannizzaro, Sarah Ader, Irwin Miller, Marion Herring, Paola Neve, Ilze Lemesis and Eileen McHugh.

Without their help and encouragement, this book would never have been realized. They supplied me with the stories, photographs and precious objects that line the pages of each story. They listened to my recitations and Eileen McHugh has heard every word in this book over and over and over. I am grateful for their love.

R. C. Gorman shared his home and time with me and gave permission to reproduce his art. Fruteland Jackson shared his life and photographs and a thank you goes to James Fraher for his great portrait of Fruteland. Donald J. Trump, Tony Hillerman and Billy Collins, graciously, shared their memories for this book.

Two people, however, have been with me from the very beginning. A special thanks goes to Robin Bartlett for all his assistance, his comments and critiques. My very special thanks go to the designer of this book, Chris Klimasz. His vision and his enthusiasm have turned words and stories into a thing of beauty.

Maria L. Valdemi

Mama Says

What Your Mother Says...

Place a picture of
your Mother here.

144

What Your Mother Says...

_____

_____

_____

_____

_____

_____

_____

Place a picture here.

145

Place a picture here

Place a picture here

What Your Mother Says…

Place a picture here

Place a picture here

_____

_____

_____

_____

_____

_____

_____

_____

_____

Place a picture here.

_____

_____

_____

_____

_____

_____

_____

_____

Place a picture here.

Place a picture here

What Your Mother Says...

_____

_____

_____

_____

_____

_____

_____

_____

_____

_____

_____

Place a picture here